T0339911

Understanding and Teaching Reflexive Sentences in Spanish

Understanding and Teaching Reflexive Sentences in Spanish provides a fresh, simple, and novel approach to understanding and teaching the use of the intransitivizing *se*.

Understanding reflexive sentences can be challenging for learners of Spanish. Instead of expecting learners to memorize multiple rules, the author offers one simple rule that allows learners to intuitively understand and use reflexive sentences. Sample exercises for students at all levels of language proficiency are also provided to practice and internalize the new approach.

This book will be of interest to teachers and learners of any second language, as well as linguists interested in second language acquisition or in second language teaching or pedagogy.

Luis H. González is Professor of Spanish and Linguistics at Wake Forest University. He completed his Ph.D. at the University of California, Davis. His main areas of research are semantic roles, case, reflexivization, clitic doubling, differential object marking, dichotomies in languages, Spanish linguistics, and second language learning. He is the co-author of *Gramática para la composición* (Georgetown University Press), a Spanish advanced grammar and writing textbook, now in its third edition (2016). He is also the author of *Cómo entender y cómo enseñar* por *y* para (Routledge, 2020), *Four Dichotomies in Spanish: Adjective Position, Adjectival Clauses, Ser/ Estar, and Preterite/Imperfect* (Routledge, 2021), and *The Fundamentally Simple Logic of Language: Learning a Second Language with the Tools of the Native Speaker* (Routledge, 2021).

Understanding and Teaching Reflexive Sentences in Spanish

Luis H. González

Spanish List Advisor: Javier Muñoz-Basols

Routledge
Taylor & Francis Group

LONDON AND NEW YORK

First published 2022
by Routledge
4 Park Square, Milton Park, Abingdon, Oxon OX14 4RN

and by Routledge
605 Third Avenue, New York, NY 10158

Routledge is an imprint of the Taylor & Francis Group, an informa business

British Library Cataloguing-in-Publication Data
A catalogue record for this book is available from the British Library

Library of Congress Cataloging-in-Publication Data
A catalog record for this book has been requested

ISBN: 978-1-032-10187-3 (hbk)
ISBN: 978-1-032-10188-0 (pbk)
ISBN: 978-1-003-21409-0 (ebk)

DOI: 10.4324/9781003214090

Typeset in Times New Roman
by Apex Covantage, LLC

To Ana, my wife, for whom this is her favorite part of my research program.

Contents

Tables

Acknowledgments

A good number of students, friends, and colleagues have contributed to this book over the years. Some of them did so by their choice, but most of them by invitation. All of them contributed in ways they can hardly imagine. The book is better thanks to all of you!

Allie Blum, Annie Wheat, Audrey Dyer, Kate McLeod, and Mary Friedman, in alphabetical order by first name, each read parts of this book or the whole book. More than one of them read it three times. Annie Wheat (AKA Annie Sweet) read the original manuscript six years ago when it was just a ten-page draft. Kate read it in 2020. Allie in 2021. Mary Friedman, one of my colleagues at Wake Forest University, read the first version of this book five or six years ago. She also read the final version of the book twice just during the last week before this manuscript went to press. Audrey read chapters at a time during the last two years.

The examples in ten different languages in Chapter 5 come also from students, colleagues, and friends, some of them going back 15 years. I will not be specific regarding the number of years out of respect for them. Natalia Azarova, a former student, did the sentences in Russian. She, like many others who helped, answered several questions. Laia Vancells López did Catalan; Judy Kem, French; Sofia Rothberger-Krall, German (with the help of a native speaker, who double-checked her sentences); Silvia Tiboni-Craft, Italian; Hosun Kim, Korean; Jessie Craft, Latin; Boženna Furmanek and Olgierda Furmanek (mother and daughter), Polish; Rafael Lima, Portuguese; and Gabriela Cerghedean, Romanian. I wanted to have some languages from other parts of the world. I tried, but was not completely successful. I got some sentences from Fongbe, but it was too late to include them. Those languages will be represented in a book on datives that is in the works. Lovely speaking with you, Lucien (Houenou), for a couple of hours! Looking forward to our next conversation! Since my initial efforts to find some sentences in other languages to match the 11 types of "reflexive" sentences in Spanish were not promising at the beginning of the last two months of writing this book, I turned to research and included some languages from Africa, Asia, and Central America. Those languages are presented at the end of Chapter 5.

All of the three reviewers for this book had wonderful feedback. Some of their corrections and suggestions improved this manuscript. They anticipated several questions that readers would have asked. I tried to answer some of them. I can honestly say that those reviews were written with true love, and for that, I am infinitely thankful. Those reviews were so helpful, that if reviewers do not get a free copy of the book for doing so, I will see to it (through Samantha Vale-Noya, my wonderful editor at Routledge, who also deserves praise for bringing this project to completion) that each of the reviewers gets a copy. If need be, on me!

Thanks to all of those who shared their love in this book in one way or another. The most rewarding part of having something or owning something is sharing it. Knowledge that is not shared does not really exist. This book is about the love for learning and the love of sharing, and it is not my work alone. I have simply compiled the knowledge and love that have been shared with me.

Wake Forest University, August 4, 2021.

1 Subject and direct object or <u>verber</u> and verbed?

1.1. Introduction

González (2021) provides ample evidence that children understand and use SUBJECT and DIRECT OBJECT in any sentence not because they have learned or have an implicit knowledge of these two grammatical relations. He argues that in a sentence like (1a) below, *Ángela* is expressed as the subject and *a letter* as the direct object because speakers are intuitively and implicitly computing two simple entailments: a <u>VERBER</u> ENTAILMENT and a **VERBED** ENTAILMENT. If (1a) is true, then, which of the sentences in (1b-e) are true?[1]

(1) a. <u>Ángela</u> sent **a letter**.
    b. <u>Ángela</u> was the sender.
    c. #<u>Ángela</u> was the sent.[2]
    d. #**A letter** was the sender.
    e. **A letter** was (the) sent.

If (1a) is true, the sentences in (1b,e) are also true. The sentence in (1b) is the <u>VERBER</u> ENTAILMENT; the one in (2e) is the **VERBED** ENTAILMENT. They are logical entailments that follow necessarily if (1a) is true. Of course, (1c,d) are not true if (1a) is true.

With the <u>verber</u> and **verbed** entailments, we understand why speakers of any language will say the equivalent of *Linguists propose the coolest theories all the time* and why no speaker says in any language the equivalent of *The coolest theories propose linguists all the time*. The following section shows that <u>verber</u> and **verbed** are not just a different label for subject and direct object.

DOI: 10.4324/9781003214090-1

1.2. How *verbed* reveals a difference that *subject* hides

Let us now consider two sentences with just one participant. This participant is always the subject. However, we will see that the subject can be the <u>verber</u> or the **verbed**:

(2) a. <u>Ángela</u> studied.
    b. **Taxes** were increased.
    c. **Taxes** increased.

Let us apply the <u>verber</u> entailment and the **verbed** entailment to these sentences:

(3) a. <u>Ángela</u> is the studier (i.e. the student).
    b. #Ángela is the studied.
    c. #Taxes were the increaser.
    d. **Taxes** were (the) increased.

It turns out that (3a) and (3d) are correct entailments from (2a-c). Those entailments show that the subject of (2a) is *Ángela* and she is the "<u>studier</u>" (student). They also show that **taxes** are the **increased**. Since the single participant in an intransitive sentence is the subject, observe that the subject of (2b,c) is the increased, not the increaser. That is, the <u>VERBER</u> ENTAILMENT and the **VERBED** ENTAILMENT show that the subject of a sentence can be the <u>verber</u> or the **verbed**.

Sentences (2a-c) are INTRANSITIVE because they have just one participant. It seems more appropriate to call sentences (2b,c) INTRANSITIVIZED than intransitive. These two sentences are a syntactic variation of the transitive sentence, *<u>the government</u> increased **taxes***. The latter is the underlying sentence called the active voice sentence. Sentence (2b) is the passive voice alternation. We will call sentences like (2c) intransitivized sentences from now on.

Those familiar with scholarly work on reflexive sentences know that sentence (2c) is a DECAUSATIVE sentence (a sentence whose causer has been omitted). That term will not be used again until Chapter 5, where it will become clear for those unfamiliar with it.

TRANSITIVE: a sentence is transitive if it has a <u>verber</u> and a **verbed** (González 2021: 6).

INTRANSITIVE: a sentence is intransitive (or INTRANSITIVIZED) if it has just a <u>verber</u> or a **verbed**, but not both.

Now we are ready to propose that native speakers determine who or what is the subject and who or what is the direct object in a sentence by applying the following rule (González 2021: 6):

(4) Verber and **Verbed** Argument Selection Principle (VVASP):[3]
     The participant in a sentence that passes the verber entailment is
     expressed as the subject; the participant that passes the **verbed**
     entailment is expressed as the direct object of a transitive sentence, but
     as the subject of a sentence without a verber.

ARGUMENT is the specialized term in linguistics and philosophy for
the "core" participants in a sentence. In terms of this book, verber, **verbed**,
and verbee are the traditional arguments. Other participants are ADJUNTS.
Arguments are presumably "selected" by the verb. Adjuncts are more freely
added or deleted.

Up to this point, we have seen what transitive, intransitive, and intransitivized sentences are. A transitive sentence has a verber and a **verbed**; an
intransitive sentence has a verber or a **verbed**, but not both; an intransitivized
sentence is a sentence from which either its verber or its **verbed** was omitted.
An important point of this way of understanding subject and direct object is
that the subject of an intransitive (or an intransitivized) sentence can be the
verber or the **verbed**, a difference that the notion of subject has blurred for
over 21 centuries. For example, the subject of all sentences in the passive
voice is a **verbed**. The subject of UNACCUSATIVE verbs (*belong, cost,
happen, matter, occur, remain, seem*, etc.) is the **verbed**. See González (2021:
Chapter 5), for a discussion of the true *gustar* verbs in Spanish (the equivalent in Spanish of verbs like *belong, happen*, etc.). As this book shows, the
subject of sentences with a "reflexive" pronoun is the **verbed** or the verbee.

UNACCUSATIVE verbs are verbs whose only object has to be an indirect object, like *pertenecer* 'belong', *gustar* 'like', *ocurrir* 'happen/occur',
etc. They are verberless, but not subjectless. In the absence of a verber in
a sentence, the **verbed** is "promoted" to subject position. See González
(2021: Chapters 4 and 5).

1.3. Sentences with three participants

Consider now sentence (5) in English:

(5) We sent Grandma **our children**.

It is uncontroversial who the sender is (*we*). Is it clear who the sent is? Is
Grandma the sent or are *the children* the sent? Sentences (6a,b) will help readers who are not sure. The sentence in (5) is synonymous only with one of them:

(6) a. We sent **our children** to Grandma.
     b. #We sent Grandma to our children.

Sentences (5) and (6a) are synonymous. The sent in (5) and in (6a) are *the children*. Then, who or what is *Grandma*? *Grandma* is the beneficiary of the event of sending someone to her. *Grandma* is the beneficiary not only in (6a) but also in (5).

As González (2021: 11) shows, the indirect object is the participant who benefits or suffers some harm as a result from the event expressed in a sentence. For this reason, we will refer to the INDIRECT OBJECT as the BENEFICIARY (or MALEFICIARY). Gil (1982: 122) called the participant expressed as an indirect object of the equivalent in Hebrew of verbs like *belong, be born, matter, happen, seem* the *benefactee* or the *malefactee*. A fitting generalization for benefactee and malefactee is VERBEE (see González 2021: Chapter 1). The reader is invited to determine verber, **verbed**, and verbee in the following sentences. Please do not proceed with the reading if you would like to do the exercise before reading the answers.

(7) a. We sent a beautiful bouquet of flowers to Grandma.
   b. We sent Grandma a beautiful bouquet of flowers.
   c. A beautiful bouquet of flowers was sent to Grandma (by us).
   d. Grandma was sent a beautiful bouquet of flowers.

It is uncontroversial that *we* is the sender; *a beautiful bouquet of flowers* is the sent, and *Grandma* is the benefactee (verbee), regardless of the fact that *we* can be the subject (7a,b), a "*by phrase*" (7c), or it can be left out altogether (7d). *A beautiful bouquet of flowers* can be the direct object (7a,d), the secondary object (7b), or the subject (7c). Grandma can be the indirect object (7a,c), the primary object (7b), or the subject (7d). Thus, verber, **verbed**, and verbee are constant and more easily identifiable than subject, direct object, and indirect object in variations of the same sentence, whereas subject, direct object, and indirect object vary and are more difficult to identify.

This book will have exercises for Chapters 2–4. Readers are referred to González (2021: Chapter 1) for exercises to practice verber, **verbed**, and verbee.

The rest of this book proposes a radically new way of understanding sentences with a "reflexive" pronoun. This proposal is based on evidence that speakers understand and produce language through their grasp of verber, **verbed**, and verbee. Until now, analyses of sentences with a "reflexive" pronoun have required the learning of ten to 15 "functions" of *se* (Ávila López-Pedraza 2009; Mendikoetxea 1999; RAE 2010; Ramsey [1894]1956; Whitley 2002; among many others). Those functions are extremely difficult to keep apart. Furthermore, those analyses fail to account for impersonal *se* sentences. The present analysis proposes a single rule of VERBER

INTRANSITIVIZATION that accounts for the 11 types of sentences with a "reflexive" pronoun in Whitley (2002: 173–184). Many scholars have proposed similar types of sentences for Spanish and for many other languages.

Notes

1 Throughout this book, the <u>verber</u> will be <u>underlined</u>; the **verbed** will be in **bold**; and the <u>verbee</u> (the indirect object) will be <u>double underlined</u>.

  Specialized or key terms are written in CAPITAL LETTERS the first time they appear or when their mention is particularly relevant. Capitalized terms will be explained briefly as needed, either in the text itself or in endnotes like this one. The first term briefly explained is ENTAILMENT.

  ENTAILMENT: a sentence B is an entailment from sentence A if every time that A is true, B is also true. This definition is based on Huddleston & Pullum (2002: 35).

  Specialized terms that are very common are not explained. Thus, SUBJECT and DIRECT OBJECT are not explained, but NOMINATIVE and ACCUSATIVE (the specialized term for each of these two terms will be explained).

2 Note: The notation "#" means not entailed or semantically anomalous. It, like the definition of ENTAILMENT provided in endnote 1, comes also from Huddleston & Pullum (2002: 35). Traditionally, an asterisk before a sentence (*) indicates that the sentence is ungrammatical. It might be preferable to agree that an asterisk indicates a sentence that is never or rarely used by native speakers in their normal use of language. Maldonado ([1999]2006: 43) uses a double question mark (??) to flag *casos marginales* 'marginal cases'. This author will stick with an asterisk in this book to indicate a sentence never or rarely used by native speakers in their normal use of language. Carlota de Benito Moreno told this author (PC, 2021) that she used double question marks in her doctoral dissertation and has used them in her writing because she has found in corpora sentences that she thought native speakers would not produce.

3 This argument selection principle comes from González (2021: 6). It is modelled after the Argument Selection Principle in Dowty (1991: 576).

References

Ávila López-Pedraza, Julio. 2009. Análisis de los usos de *se* desde la gramática descriptiva. *Hispania* 92.791–799. www.jstor.org/stable/40648461.

Dowty, David. 1991. Thematic proto-roles and argument selection. *Language* 67.547–619. www.jstor.org/stable/pdf/415037.

Gil, David. 1982. Case marking, phonological size, and linear order. In Hopper, Paul & Thompson, Sandra A. (eds.), *Studies in transitivity. Syntax and semantics 15.* 117–140.

González, Luis H. 2021. *The fundamentally simple logic of language: Learning a second language with the tools of the native speaker.* London: Routledge.

Huddleston, Rodney & Pullum, Geoffrey K. 2002. *The Cambridge grammar of the English language.* Cambridge: Cambridge University Press.

Maldonado, Ricardo. [1999]2006. *A media voz. Problemas conceptuales del clítico se.* México, DF: Universidad Nacional Autónoma de México.

Mendikoetxea, Amaya. 1999. Construcciones con *se*: Medias, pasivas e impersonales. In Bosque, Ignacio & Demonte Barreto, Violeta (eds.), *Gramática descriptiva de la lengua española*, vol. 2, 1631–1722. Madrid: Espasa Calpe S.A.

RAE (Real Academia Española y Asociación de Academias de la Lengua Española).
2010. *Nueva gramática de la lengua española. Manual.* Bogotá: Editorial Planeta
Colombiana S.A.

Ramsey, Marathon. [1894]1956. *A textbook of modern Spanish.* New York: Holt,
Reinhart and Winston. (Revised by Robert Spaulding).

Whitley, M. Stanley. 2002. *Spanish/English contrasts. A course in Spanish linguistics.* 2nd edn. Washington, DC: Georgetown University Press.

2 Turning reflexivization on its head

2.1. Introduction

In addition to true reflexive sentences with a direct object (*Bernardo se afeitó* 'Bernardo shaved himself') and reflexive sentences with an indirect object (*Bernardo se cortó un dedo* 'Bernardo cut his finger'), Spanish has as many as ten to 15 different constructions with a reflexive pronoun. However, most of them are not reflexive in meaning. Those structures are described in a list of functions of *se* (the most frequent form of a reflexive pronoun) on which not even scholars can agree, because some of those structures are poorly understood by many.[1] Scholars (and teachers trying to explain reflexive constructions in Spanish) realize that "function" *x* behaves like "function" *y* in some respects but not in others (Ávila López-Pedraza 2009: 794; Whitley 2002: 177). The functions of *se* are a formidable challenge not only for students of Spanish as a second language but also for native speakers and even for scholars. This chapter shows that a rule of <u>VERBER</u> INTRANSITIVIZATION explains these functions in such a way that learners of Spanish as a second language can reach an understanding of intransitivizing pronouns ("reflexive" pronouns) that has eluded them, and even scholars, for centuries. Moreover, <u>verber</u> intransitivization is a single rule that brings order to the, until now, unruly reflexive constructions in Spanish. This analysis can easily apply to other languages. Chapter 5 offers examples of sentences intransitivized with a reflexive pronoun in approximately 30 different languages.[2]

Se is used throughout the book to stand for the corresponding reflexive pronoun in each sentence. It is also the most frequent reflexive pronoun and the form for five out of nine different possible grammatical slots, as Table 2.1 below shows. The other forms of the reflexive pronoun in Spanish are *me, te, nos,* and *os.*

DOI: 10.4324/9781003214090-2

INTRANSITIVIZATION is the expression of a transitive sentence as an intransitive one. Remember that if a sentence is transitive when it has a <u>verber</u> and a **verbed**, then it is predicted that a sentence without its <u>verber</u> will be intransitive (or intransitivized).

Table 2.1 Reflexive pronouns in Spanish

	Subject pronouns	Reflexive pronouns
I	yo	me (myself)
you (informal)	tú	te (yourself)
you (formal)	usted	se (yourself)
he	él	se (himself)
she	ella	se (herself)
we	nosotros/nosotras	nos (ourselves)
you (informal)	vosotros/vosotras	os (yourselves)
you (formal)	ustedes	se (yourselves)
they	ellos/ellas	se (themselves)

2.2. Reflexivization: more than meets the eye

The traditional analysis of reflexive constructions is based on the intuition that in a sentence in which the direct object is identical to the subject, the direct object must be replaced with a reflexive pronoun. Thus, the hypothetical sentence in (1a) undergoes a mandatory rule of reflexivization, as in (1b). Strikethrough indicates that that participant is replaced with the corresponding reflexive pronoun.

(1) a. **Estela vistió ~~a Estela~~*.
     **Estela dressed ~~Estela~~*.
   b. *Estela **se** vistió*.
     Estela herself dressed
     '<u>Estela</u> dressed (**herself**)'; '<u>Estela</u> got dressed'.

(Remember that the notation "*" means a sentence that native speakers never use or rarely use in their normal use of language).

In order to account for (1b), we will need a rule of DIRECT OBJECT REFLEXIVIZATION. In traditional Spanish grammar (and presumably in the grammar of many languages), the reflexive pronoun replaces the ACCUSATIVE or the DATIVE (Bello [1847]1941: 198–199, 237) when that accusative or dative is identical to the subject.[3] That observation can be traced back to Latin, in which reflexive means "bending back", the intuition that the reflexive pronoun refers to a previously mentioned noun that is not repeated but replaced with the corresponding reflexive pronoun. This traditional analysis was formalized in linguistic theory in Principle A of Binding Theory (Chomsky 1993: 188). According to that principle, <u>Estela</u> is the ANTECEDENT of *se* (*se* is a pronominal copy of **Estela**), and therefore *se* is there to avoid a second mention of **Estela**. A grammar based on the <u>verber</u> and **verbed** entailments will instead employ the notion of <u>verber</u> intransitivization. (See endnote 3 for a brief explanation of ACCUSATIVE, DATIVE, AND ANTECEDENT).

Spanish (like many languages) not only has a rule of direct object reflexivization, but also a rule of indirect object reflexivization. When the indirect object is identical to the subject, presumably the former must be replaced with a reflexive pronoun, a rule very similar to the rule that results in sentences like (1b).

(2) a. **Estela <u>le</u> puso **desodorante** ~~a Estela~~*.
   Estela DAT-pronoun put-past deodorant to Estela-DAT[4]
   'Estela put **deodorant** on (Estela)'.
   b. *Estela <u>se</u> puso **desodorante***.
   Estela REFL put-past deodorant
   'Estela put **deodorant** on'.
   (cf. **Estela puso **desodorante***; *'Estela put **deodorant**').

To account for the sentence in (2b), we will need a rule of INDIRECT OBJECT REFLEXIVIZATION that will replace the indirect object with a reflexive pronoun when the indirect object is identical to the subject. In terms of a grammar based on the <u>verber</u> and **verbed** entailments, this will be a rule of <u>VERBEE</u> reflexivization. So far, we need two rules to account for two types of reflexive sentences.

Note that the *se* is not merely a way of avoiding an unwanted repetition, but a signal that the **verbed** or the <u>verbee</u> has been replaced, and *se* is left as a TRACE. TRACE has a specialized meaning in linguistics. Rather than offering a specialized definition, it suffices to say that a PRONOUN is a TRACE (i.e., a copy) of a noun (plus modifiers) that has been replaced. That pronoun helps listeners/readers keep track of who does what to whom in a sentence, the heart of language understanding and production. As this author explains it to students, direct object, indirect object, reflexive, and prepositional pronouns are TRACKING clues (tags) in languages.

The next section turns the explanation in (1a,b) and (2a,b) upside down.

2.3. Reflexivization turned upside down

Let us consider the "passive *se*" sentence in (3b) from Spanish:

(3) a. ~~*Blum Construction*~~ *remodeló* **este edificio**.
     'Blum Construction remodeled **this building**'.
   b. **Este edificio** *se remodeló*.
      This building REFL-pronoun remodeled
      'This building was remodeled'.
   c. **Este edificio** fue remodelado.   (Passive voice in Spanish)
      '**This building** was remodeled'.   (Passive voice in English)
   d. #*Blum Construction se remodeló*.
   e. #'Blum Construction remodeled itself'.   (#'Blum Construction was
                                                  remodeled'.)

Remember that the notation "#" means not entailed or semantically anomalous (Huddleston & Pullum 2002: 35).

Sentence (3b) is called a passive *se* sentence; sentence (3c) is called a passive with *ser* 'be' plus the past participle of the main verb (a sentence in the passive voice). Sentences (3b) and (3c) are synonyms, but Spanish prefers passive *se* sentences to passives with *ser* (see §4.2 for an explanation). In order to account for (3b), we would need a rule of subject reflexivization. This is the third rule. In our terms, we will need a rule of <u>VERBER REFLEXIVIZATION</u>. Notice that (1b) and (2b) are truly reflexive in meaning, but (3b) is not; it is reflexive only in form. The *se*, which is either required or favored (depending on the verb), indicates to the listener or reader that the building is the **remodeled**, as (3b) shows for Spanish and the glosses for (3b,c) show for English. In fact, instead of calling a rule that accounts for (3b) a rule of <u>Verber</u> Reflexivization, it is more appropriate to call it a rule of <u>VERBER</u> INTRANSITIVIZATION. It is uncontroversial that (3b) is an intransitivized sentence and it is clearly not a reflexive sentence. Sentence (3c) is indisputably an intransitivized sentence, and so is (3b). No building remodels itself; buildings get remodeled by builders.

If a rule of direct object reflexivization were correct, it would predict that #*Blum Construction se remodeló* is true if the sentence *Blum Construction remodeló* **este edificio** is true. Current rules for direct and indirect object reflexivization predict the incorrect entailment in (3d) and fail to predict the correct one in (3b). A rule of <u>VERBER</u> INTRANSITIVIZATION predicts that if (3a) is true, speakers of Spanish will say sentences like (3b), that (3b) and (3c) should be synonymous, and that speakers of Spanish will not say sentences like (3d). All of these predictions are evidence that a rule of <u>verber</u> intransitivization is a good explanation for sentence (3b). A rule of <u>verber</u> intransitivization also explains the similarities between a passive with *se* (3b) and a passive with *ser* 'be' (3c).

Sentence (4) below is a famous type of sentence in many languages, commonly called IMPERSONAL PASSIVE (Perlmutter & Postal 1983: 107). Permutter and Postal also observed that these sentences are possible only with sentences whose only participant is agentive. In our terms, possible with sentences whose only argument is a <u>verber</u>.[5] They are called impersonal *se* sentences in Spanish grammar.

(4) *Aquí se trabaja mucho.*
    'Here <u>one/you/people</u> work(s) a lot'.

Our current understanding of reflexivization would not lead anyone to seek a connection between sentence (4) and sentences (1–3), and as far as this author knows, nobody has done so. The <u>verber</u>/**verbed** entailments would prompt an attentive reader to look at this construction in a different way. So-called impersonal *se* is <u>verber</u> replacement with a reflexive pronoun. This appears counterintuitive vis-à-vis sentences (1) and (2), but it makes perfect sense vis-à-vis sentence (3). Observe how the *se* is replacing the <u>verber</u> as in (3b). Observe also that if there is neither a <u>verber</u> nor a **verbed** in a sentence, the sentence is ungrammatical, as (5c) shows:

(5) a. *Aquí* ~~*la gente/uno/tú/usted*~~ *trabaja mucho.*   (*tú*: informal; *usted*: formal)
       here ~~people/one/you/you~~ work(s) a lot
       'Here people/one/you/you work(s) a lot'.
    b. *Aquí se trabaja mucho.*
    c. *Aquí trabaja mucho.

If we need a rule of <u>VERBER</u> INTRANSITIVIZATION to explain sentence (3b), and if it looks like the same rule accounts for (4), let us turn (1) and (2) upside down and try to explain them with a rule of <u>VERBER</u> INTRANSITIVIZATION, as in (6) below. Strikethrough indicates that the participant is replaced with the corresponding reflexive pronoun.

(6) a. ~~*Estela*~~ *vistió **a Estela**.*
    b. ***Estela** se vistió.*   (<u>verber</u> intransitivization)
    c. ~~*Estela*~~ *le puso **desodorante** a Estela.*
    d. ~~*Estela*~~ *se puso **desodorante**.*   (<u>verber</u> intransitivization)

The resulting sentences are exactly as if we were doing direct object or indirect object reflexivization. Nothing is lost. Let us begin counting the gains.

First, instead of three different rules to explain sentences (1–3), we need only one rule. Second, there is no need for the counterintuitive "impersonal *se*", because a rule of verber intransitivization explains this construction as well.[6] That is four sentences with the same rule. From now on, neither native speakers nor second language learners of Spanish will have to learn "impersonal *se*", an unnecessary piece of language trivia. No learner of many different languages, for that matter, will have to do so.

In addition to these two significant simplifications in the grammar (reducing four rules to one, and no longer having a need for learning "impersonal *se*" sentences), what is the evidence that the nominative (the subject) of the reflexive sentence in (6b) is **Estela** (the **verbed**) and not Estela (the verber)?

First, examine sentence (3b) (the sentence of this building being remodeled by Blum Construction). Observe that a passive *se* sentence is equivalent to passive voice (passive with *ser* 'be'): *este edificio se remodeló = este edificio fue remodelado* 'this building was/got remodeled'. Thus, passive voice of a direct object is evidence that the **Estela** in preverbal position in (6b) is the **verbed**.

Second, reflexivization in a sentence in which the indirect object is identical to the subject. What is the evidence that the grammatical subject is not the verber Estela, as in (7b), but the verbee Estela, promoted to subject, as in (7c)? In other words, what is the evidence that the subject is not the original Estela, as in (7b), but Estela, who was promoted from indirect object to subject, as in (7c)?

(7) a. **Estela le puso **desodorante** a Estela.*
     b. *Estela se puso **desodorante**.*
        (Estela is the original verber; *se* is replacing Estela)
     c. *Estela se puso **desodorante**.*
        (The new subject is the initial verbee, promoted to subject. *Se* is replacing Estela).

There is evidence in English, as (8c) below shows:

(8) a. The Swedish Academy gave **the Nobel Prize** to Vargas Llosa.
     b. **The Nobel Prize** was given to Vargas Llosa.   (Unaccusativization)
     c. Vargas Llosa was given **the Nobel Prize**.   (Undativization)

Sentence (8b) is a passive voice sentence. In terms of this proposal, it is a **verbed** promoted to subject. Passive morphology (*was verbed*) indicates to the listener or reader that *the Nobel Prize* was the **given**, not the <u>giver</u>. If the expression of a **verbed** in subject position is aptly called an UNACCU-SATIVIZATION (the accusative – DO – unaccusativizes, and is promoted to be the subject of the sentence), it would be equally apt to call (8c) an UNDATIVIZATION; that is, a promotion of the dative to the nominative (indirect object to subject). Now not only linguists but many college (and even high school) students will understand why this is a rule of undativiza-tion, since the dative, i.e., the indirect object is promoted to the nomina-tive (the subject) in the sentence. Who/what is missing in (8c)? The <u>verber</u>. And we all know that <u>Vargas Llosa</u> will not be giving the Nobel Prize to anyone. <u>Vargas Llosa</u> keeps being <u>the benefactee</u> because he was given the Nobel Prize and because subject, direct object, and indirect object change, but <u>verber</u>, **verbed**, and <u>verbee</u> remain constant in different alternations of a sentence. Since reflexivization is so strong in Romance languages, it is not surprising that the equivalent of the undativization in sentences like (8c) is done in these languages with a reflexive pronoun, which is a "passivizing" (an intransitivizing) pronoun in Spanish (and presumably in other languages belonging to different families), more than passive voice with *ser* 'be' plus the past participle of the main verb. Let us exemplify with Spanish. We will see a reflexive pronoun, but the meaning is not reflexive at all. Vargas Llosa will not be given to anyone, nor can Vargas Llosa give anyone the Nobel Prize. It will always be true, however, that Vargas Llosa was given the Nobel Prize.

(9) a. *<u>La Academia Sueca</u> le dio **el Premio Nóbel** <u>a Vargas Llosa</u>.*
     '<u>The Swedish Academy</u> gave **the Nobel Prize** to Vargas Llosa'.
   b. ***El Premio Nóbel** <u>le</u> fue dado <u>a Vargas Llosa</u>.*
     '**The Nobel Prize** was given to Vargas Llosa'.
   c. *<u>Se le</u> dio **el Premio Nóbel** <u>a Vargas Llosa</u>.* = "unplanned
                                        occurrence"[7]
     '**The Nobel Prize** was given to Vargas Llosa'.
   d. *<u>A Vargas Llosa</u> <u>se</u> <u>le</u> dio **el Premio Nóbel**.* = TOPICALIZATION of
                                        the IO[8]
     '<u>Vargas Llosa</u> was given **the Nobel Prize**'.

Let us briefly explain TOPICALIZATION, UNACCUSATIVIZATION, and UNDATIVIZATION. TOPICALIZATION is the expression of the indi-rect object (or the direct object) before the verb. The subject is commonly called the TOPIC of the sentence. When the direct object or the indirect object is expressed before the verb, it has been topicalized; that is, turned into the topic of the sentence. Passive voice is a form of topicalization as well. As for UNACCUSATIVIZATION, a direct object "unaccusativizes" when it loses its accusative status (its mark as an accusative) and is expressed as the subject (the nominative) in the sentence. Passive voice sentences and passives with *se* are unaccusativizations. Sentences (8b) and (9b) are unaccusativizations. UNDATIVIZATION is the expression of an indirect object (the dative) before the verb. An indirect object "undativizes" when it loses its dative status (its mark as a dative) and is expressed as the subject (the nominative) in the sentence. Sentence (8c) is an undativization in English.

Sentences (8c) and (9d) are also called indirect object topicalization in English and Spanish, a very desirable coincidence for the purposes of understanding the grammar of each language. In addition, the same sentence but with a different word order is what we see in (9c), a sentence called in textbooks for Spanish "the unplanned or accidental *SE*". This sentence is simply <u>verber</u> intransitivization of a sentence with **verbed** and <u>verbee</u>. Since indirect object and "reflexive" pronouns are both robust phenomena in the grammar of Spanish, this sentence is as "Spanishy" as it can be. "Spanishy" is a term this author began to use in his teaching to show students how a sentence might be expressed in Spanish rather than a word-by-word translation from another language. For example, *me lavé el pelo* 'I washed my hair' is "Spanishy" because that is the sentence that a native speaker will utter. On the other hand, ??*lavé mi pelo* is a calque from English. No native speaker of English says a sentence like ??*I washed myself the hair*, with the intended meaning that you washed your hair, and that your hair is still attached to your head.

Remember that the notation "??" is used by Maldonado ([1999]2006: 43) for *casos marginales* 'marginal cases'. It seems appropriate in this case.

Third, there is evidence for a rule of <u>verber</u> intransitivization in CAUSATIVE sentences, which means that there is evidence for this analysis in a large number of languages. In a CAUSATIVE sentence, you make someone do something for you. For example, the most common interpretation of (10a) is that Rosa had her hair cut by someone else, as (10b) shows. It is also possible that she cut it herself, as (10c) shows.

(10) a. <u>*Rosa*</u> <u>*se*</u> *cortó **el pelo***.
       Rosa REFL-pronoun cut-past the hair
       'Rosa cut **her hair**' (with the meaning <u>Rosa</u> had **her hair** cut).
    b. *<u>Un peluquero</u> <u>le</u> cortó **el pelo** <u>a Rosa</u>.*
       a hair stylist DAT-pronoun cut-past the hair to Rosa-DAT
       'A hair stylist cut Rosa's **hair**'.
    c. **<u>Rosa</u> <u>le</u> cortó **el pelo** <u>a Rosa</u>.*
       Rosa REFL-pronoun cut-past the hair to Rosa-DAT
       (A hypothetical sentence that must undergo <u>verber</u> intransitivization)
    d. <u>Rosa</u> <u>se</u> cortó **el pelo**.
       'Rosa cut her hair'.

There are at least three very important observations to be drawn from the sentences in (10). First, the traditional analysis of reflexivization as replacement of the indirect object predicts that these two sentences are arrived at by applying two different rules. In the reflexive interpretation (derived from 10c), there would be a rule of indirect object reflexivization. In the causative construction (derived from 10b), there would be a rule of subject reflexivization. The second observation is that the analysis proposed here not only reduces those two different rules to a single rule of <u>verber</u> intransitivization (that is already part of the grammar) but also predicts the ambiguity in <u>*Rosa* <u>*se*</u> *cortó*</u> *el pelo*. This is by virtue of the fact that the same rule can apply to a sentence with two different <u>verbers</u>. The first interpretation is the causative one in which she had <u>someone else</u> cut **her hair** for her (similar to <u>Vargas Llosa</u> having been given **the Nobel Prize**); the second is the truly reflexive one in which <u>Rosa</u> cut <u>herself</u> **her hair**. The third observation is that the causative interpretation is the intended interpretation most of the time, and it clearly shows that the grammatical subject is the underlying indirect object (<u>Rosa</u>), not the subject (<u>el peluquero</u>). And we can be sure that <u>Rosa</u> is the underlying indirect object (the <u>benefactee</u> of the haircut) because the <u>verber</u> is the hair stylist. Many languages in the world have causative constructions like this one.

To summarize thus far, the main point of "reflexivization" is not "true reflexivization"; it is INTRANSITIVIZATION. In fact, textbook writers and linguists should start calling reflexive pronouns intransitivizing pronouns. Here is a summary of the discussion thus far, and why <u>verber</u> intransitivization is a better name for this phenomenon than reflexivization. As Chapter 3 will show, reflexivization is always intransitivization, but most of the time intransitivization does not result in "reflexivization". Reflexivization has hidden the true power of intransitivization the same way that the notion of subject has hidden the observation that the subject is often the **verbed** (or the <u>verbee</u>), not the <u>verber</u>. Let us summarize three reasons why "reflexive" pronouns should be called intransitivizing pronouns.

First, in terms of direct object and indirect object, a ditransitive sentence becomes transitive when a reflexive pronoun shows that the <u>verber</u> has been omitted.

(11) a. <u>*La Academia Sueca* <u>*le*</u> dio **el Premio Nóbel** <u>*a Vargas Llosa*</u>.</u>
    The academy swedish DAT-pronoun gave the prize nobel to
    Vargas Llosa-DAT
    '<u>The Swedish Academy</u> gave **the Nobel Prize** <u>to Vargas Llosa</u>'.

   b. <u>*Se* <u>*le*</u> dio **el Premio Nóbel** <u>*a Vargas Llosa*</u>.</u>
    REFL-pronoun DAT-pronoun gave the prize nobel to Vargas
    Llosa-DAT
    '**The Nobel Prize** was given <u>to Vargas Llosa</u>'.

c. *A Vargas Llosa se le dio **el Premio Nóbel**.*
to Vargas Llosa-DAT REFL-pronoun DAT-pronoun gave the prize nobel
'Vargas Llosa was given **the Nobel Prize**'.

Sentences (11b-c) are synonymous. Sentence (11c) is indirect object topicalization, and the best equivalent in Spanish of a passive of indirect object in English (Vargas Llosa was given **the Nobel Prize**), which can also be called an indirect object topicalization. A nice encounter in the syntax of two languages belonging to two different families. An encounter that should be called verbee topicalization, if we want to use a more intuitive name. And now we can kill two birds with one stone, because it will be very easy for the reader to understand why grammarians and textbook writers might refer in the future to **verbed** topicalization and verbee topicalization, which are the same as unaccusativization and undativization, respectively.

Second, a transitive sentence becomes intransitive (i.e. unaccusativizes) when an intransitivizing pronoun shows that the verber has been omitted:

(12) a. *Los papás llamaron **a esta niña** Cecilia.*
'Her parents called this girl Cecilia'.
b. ***Esta niña** se llama Cecilia.*
'This girl is called Cecilia'.

(See §4.2 for a more detailed explanation of how telling your name in Spanish – and in other languages – is an intransitivization with *se*).

Third, even an intransitive sentence can be intransitivized if a reflexive pronoun (an intransitivizing pronoun) is left in the sentence to show that the verber has been omitted:

(13) a. *En esta universidad la gente/uno/usted trabaja mucho.*
'At this university people/one/you/ work(s) a lot'.
'A lot is worked at this university'.
b. *En esta universidad se trabaja mucho.*
c. **En esta universidad trabaja mucho.*

The intransitivization in (13b) provides strong evidence for our rule of VERBER INTRANSITVIZATION. If reflexivization were replacement of the **direct object** or the indirect object with a reflexive pronoun when identical to the subject, UNERGATIVE sentences (intransitive sentences whose only participant is the verber) should not admit a "reflexive" pronoun. They do, as (13b) shows, because "reflexivization" is verber intransitivization, not direct or indirect object reflexivization, as believed by most scholars and teachers until now.

For readers less familiar with linguistics, UNERGATIVE SENTENCES are intransitive sentences whose only participant is agentive (an initial 1 in Relational Grammar, a theory after which the term unergative began to be widely used). In terms of this proposal, unergative sentences are sentences whose subject is a <u>verber</u> (*dance, sneeze, snore, swim, walk*, etc.). These are typical verbs used in impersonal passives (Perlmutter & Postal 1983: 107–112). Observe, however, that some of these verbs admit an object: *dance a waltz, walk your dog.* That is one reason why verbs are not really transitive or intransitive. In fact, most transitive verbs can be used intransitively. However, a given sentence is transitive or intransitive, but never both at the same time, as argued in González (2021: 62).

2.4. How <u>Estela</u> <u>se</u> parece a su mamá is not an idiom; it is similar to <u>Estela</u> <u>se</u> sirvió un café

This author asked at a Spanish linguistics conference, at which there were at least 15 linguists and 30 graduate students in the audience (Greenville, North Carolina, USA, on February 7th, 2015), whether anybody had seen or knew an explanation for the following sentence:

(14) *Estela se parece a la mamá.*
Estela REFL-pronoun looks like to the mother-ACC
'Stella looks like her Mom'.

There was no answer. In addition to simply a translation provided for sentence (14), this author has seen one explanation. Ávila López-Pedraza (2009: 797) offered an explanation in an exercise on the functions of *se* in his article in *Hispania*. He is an experienced teacher who felt compelled to clarify the point for other teachers.

> *Mi primo se parece mucho a nuestro abuelo. Parecerse* no se trata de verbo reflexivo (salvo en la oración: *Qué personaje es Juan: cada día se parece más a sí mismo*) en este contexto, ya que el verbo lleva un obligatorio complemento (sic) de régimen, dado que el significado de "salir a alguien" se consigue con la preposición A: *parecerse a.* Es decir, no puede parecerse a sí mismo y a la vez a su abuelo. Considerado desde otro enfoque: ¿qué significa "aparecer"? "Aparecer" significa "hacerse presente"; "parecerse a" significa "salir a alguien". El verbo cambia claramente de significado, luego *se* es un diferenciador semántico.

My cousin looks a lot like Grandpa. Look like is not a reflexive verb (except in the sentence: *What a character John is: every day looks more like himself*) in this context, since the verb carries a mandatory complement of *REGIMEN*, given that the meaning of "look like someone" is achieved with the preposition A: *look like.*[9] That is, [he] cannot look like himself and at the same time look like his Grandpa. Considered from another viewpoint: What is the meaning of "appear"? "Appear" means "to make yourself present"; "look like" means "resemble someone". The verb clearly changes meaning, then *se* is a semantic distinguisher.

(Translation by this author, LHG).

Ávila López-Pedraza confused *aparecer* 'appear' and *parecerse a* 'look like'. To be fair, explaining *parecerse a alguien* with subject, direct object, and indirect object is a daunting task. You might not look like your Grandpa, but you definitely look like yourself. <u>Verber</u> intransitivization accounts for this sentence the same way that it accounts for Rosa having her hair cut, Vargas Llosa having been awarded the Nobel Prize, and countless sentences with <u>verbee</u> topicalization in Spanish. Let us see how.

Let us use an example of serving coffee to someone else and serving some coffee for oneself so we can see better the abstraction in *parecerse a* 'look like someone', 'resemble someone' ground-ed on a less abstract example (*parecerse a* is rather abstract, but having coffee is very concrete):

(15) a. *Estela <u>le</u> sirvió **una taza de café** <u>a Luigi</u>.*
     '<u>Estela</u> served **a cup of coffee** <u>to Luigi</u>'
  b. *<u>A Luigi</u> <u>se</u> <u>le</u> sirvió **una taza de café**.*
     '<u>Luigi</u> was served **a cup of coffee**'.
  c. **<s>Estela</s> <u>le</u> sirvió **una taza de café** <u>a Estela</u>.*
  d. *Estela <u>se</u> sirvió **una taza de café**.*
     <u>Estela</u> REFL-pronoun served **a cup of coffee**
     'Estela served a cup of coffee for herself'.
     (cf. ??Estela sirvió **una taza de café**.)[10]
(16) a. *<s>Estela</s> <u>le</u> parece **a su mamá** <u>a Estela</u>.*
     Estela DAT-pronoun looks like her mother-ACC to Estela-DAT
  b. *Estela <u>se</u> parece **a su mamá**.*
     'Estela looks like her Mom'.

With <u>verber</u> intransitivization, *parecerse a* is simply another promotion of the indirect object to subject (undativization), like <u>Estela</u> putting **deodorant** <u>on</u>, putting **her coat** <u>on</u>, or <u>Grandma</u> having been sent **a beautiful bouquet of flowers**. Like all of the sentences discussed above, this is simply an intransitivization with *se* (of a sentence with verber, **verbed**, and verbee). The *a* is the accusative *a* of Spanish (differential object marking) because *su mamá* is a definite human direct object that is equivalent in this sense to a proper name, the prototypical direct object that requires accusative *a* in Spanish by virtue of being the highest ranking participant in Silverstein (1976) Animacy Hierarchy. Sentence (16b) is not an idiomatic sentence in Spanish nor is the *se* a *diferenciador semántico* (a semantic "distinguisher"), another piece of language trivia not needed to account for the mandatory presence of *se* in this example. The *se* is there to show that the verber was left out because it is identical to the verbee.

2.5. Does a reflexive pronoun replace the direct object/ indirect object or the subject?

As far as I know, no scholar of Spanish has claimed that the reflexive pronoun replaces the subject. It is hard for scholars of Spanish to go beyond the intuition that a reflexive pronoun does not replace a direct object or an indirect object that is identical to the subject.[11] Except for causative sentences (*Rosa se operó* 'Rosa was operated on'), a type of sentence whose analysis requires several layers of depth in current linguistic theories, there is no SURFACE or "visible" evidence whatsoever in Spanish to lead any scholar to question the centuries old explanation that a reflexive pronoun replaces a direct object or an indirect object that is identical to the subject. Likewise, it is hard to find a linguist who does not agree with Principle A of Binding Theory (Chomsky 1993: 188). In simple English, that principle states that the antecedent of a reflexive pronoun is the subject. In other words, a reflexive pronoun replaces the direct object or the indirect object when identical to the subject. That principle has been revisited time and time again, of course, in virtually all linguistic theories. But the main proposal, at least regarding coreference reflexives, is the same, and it is overwhelmingly accepted. Two examples. Van Valin & LaPolla (1997: 397), drawing on work in Jackendoff (1972), state the same principle in a different framework (Role and Reference Grammar), and they do so, basically, in the same terms: "the antecedent must be higher on the thematic relations hierarchy than the reflexive. The hierarchy he assumed was AGENT > LOCATION, SOURCE, GOAL > THEME". (Van Valin & LaPolla are referring to Jackendoff with "he" in the preceding quote). Haspelmath (2019: 15) formulates the same principle in terms of syntactic positions: "The antecedent must be higher on the rank scale of syntactic positions than the reflexive pronoun". His rank of scale of syntactic positions is as follows:

subject > object > oblique > within nominal > within embedded clause

Thus, the understanding that a "reflexive" pronoun replaces a direct object (or an indirect object) when identical to the subject in a sentence is almost universal. Even more universal is the understanding that in decausative sentences (*la puerta se abrió* 'the door opened'), the intransitivizing pronoun is replacing the subject or external argument (De Benito Moreno 2010; Mendikoetxea 1999; Sánchez López 2002; Whitley 2002; among many others).

To summarize these two last paragraphs, very few scholars have proposed that an intransitivizing pronoun replaces the subject. The equivalent proposal in terms of <u>verber</u>, **verbed**, and <u>verbee</u> is advanced in González (2021: Chapter 2). The proposal that an intransitivizing pronoun is replacing the <u>verber</u> will force a re-thinking of the thematic relations hierarchy and the scale of syntactic positions mentioned two paragraphs above. Since this book is primarily intended for teachers and students, that theoretical discussion is left for future research(ers).

2.6. **An intransitivizing pronoun replaces the verber, not the subject**

Readers will remember from §2.3 that a rule of subject replacement with a reflexive pronoun accounts for four different sentences in Spanish. We also showed that the <u>verber</u> entailment and the **verbed** entailment are the tools that allowed this author to see that the subject of "truly" reflexive sentences is not the "original" (the underlying) subject but the underlying direct (or indirect) object. In terms of a grammar based on <u>verber</u> and **verbed**, in sentences **with** an intransitivizing pronoun, the participant that shows agreement with the verb and that tends to be the preverbal participant is not the <u>verber</u>; it is the **verbed** or the <u>verbee</u>. It turns out that a rule of subject intransitivization is an important improvement over the ten or so different "functions" of *se* to be discussed in Chapter 3. However, a rule of <u>verber</u> intransitivization is to be preferred. In order to see why, let us assume that the rule is a rule of subject reflexivization; that is, a rule that replaces the subject (when identical to the direct object) with a reflexive pronoun:

(17) a. *Katie vistió a Katie.
        *'Katie dressed Katie'.
      b. *Katie se vistió.*
        'Katie dressed (herself)'.
      c. *Se se vistió.
        *'Herself herself dressed'.

Thus, if the rule were a rule of subject reflexivization, we apply the rule to (17a), and we get (17b). Now we can, in theory, apply the rule again to the subject of (17b). The result would be (17c), a sentence that no speaker of Spanish utters. In other words, a rule of subject reflexivization predicts that Spanish would have sentences similar to (17c). It does not.

Let us assume now that the rule is a rule of <u>verber</u> intransitivization; that is, a rule that replaces the <u>verber</u> (when identical to the **verbed**) with an intransitivizing pronoun:

(18)　a.　*<u>Katie</u> vistió a **Katie**.
　　　　　*'Katie dressed Katie'.
　　　b.　***Katie** <u>se</u> vistió.*
　　　　　'**Katie** dressed (<u>herself</u>)'.

We can certainly apply the rule of <u>verber</u> intransitivization to (18a) to get (18b). Since there is no <u>verber</u> in (18b), the rule cannot apply again. With a rule of <u>verber</u> intransitivization, we can predict that speakers of Spanish do not utter sentences like (17c). They do not. To summarize, a rule of SUBJECT intransitivization accounts ON THE SURFACE for four different sentences, as explained in §2.3.[12] However, once we go one step further and try to apply the rule again to a sentence already intransitivized, a rule of subject reflexivization leads us to predict that native speakers would utter sentences like (17c). They do not. On the other hand, a rule of <u>VERBER</u> intransitivization leads us to predict that speakers of Spanish would *not* utter sentences like (17c), and they do not. That is strong evidence to support the claim that native speakers are applying a rule of <u>verber</u> intransitivization. More importantly, sentences (17) and (18) are evidence to support the claim that speakers understand and produce language using <u>verber</u> and **verbed** and not subject and direct object. A rule that predicts the sentences that speakers utter and explains why they do not utter other sentences is a rule that captures the knowledge of the native speaker better than competing rules. A rule of <u>verber</u> intransitivization is simpler and more encompassing than current rules to explain the presence of a "reflexive" pronoun in countless sentences in Spanish and presumably in many other languages.

For a discussion of sentences similar to (17c), interested readers might want to review García (1975: 253–257). She reviews scholarly work on sentences like *se se arrepintió *'*herself herself* repented'. The explanation proposed here is simpler than the one proposed by her.

2.7.　Conclusions

This chapter shows that if a rule that presumably replaces the direct object (or the indirect) with a reflexive pronoun were correct, it would predict that #<u>Blum Construction</u> **se** *remodeló* (3d) is true if the sentence <u>Blum</u>

Construction remodeló **este edificio** (sentence 3a) is true. Current rules for direct and indirect object reflexivization predict the incorrect entailment in (3d) and fail to predict the correct one in *este edificio se remodeló* (3b). A rule of <u>VERBER</u> INTRANSITIVIZATION predicts that if (3a) is true, speakers of Spanish will say sentences like (3b), that (3b) and *este edificio fue remodelado* 'this building was remodeled' (3c) should be synonymous, and that speakers of Spanish will not say sentences like (3d). All of these predictions are evidence that a single rule of <u>verber</u> intransitivization explains (3b), truly reflexives sentences, impersonal passive sentences, and sentences like *tú te pareces a alguien de tu familia* 'you look like someone in your family'. Chapters 3 and 4 will show that an intransitivizing pronoun indicates that the "new" subject is the **verbed** or <u>verbee</u>. A rule of <u>verber</u> intransitivization also explains in a principled way why a "reflexive" pronoun is used in nonreflexive sentences (Chapter 5). In fact, as the 11 types of verber intransitivization in Chapter 3 show, "true" reflexive sentences are a special case of <u>verber</u> intransitivization and not the other way around. Most sentences with an intransitivizing pronoun are not reflexive in meaning, but all "reflexive" sentences have been intransitivized by one participant (the <u>verber</u>), which has been replaced with an intransitivizing pronoun.

2.8. Exercises

Exercise 1. Write sentences with the words given. Every verb that must be conjugated requires an intransitivizing pronoun. Learners should think why an intransitivizing pronoun is mandatory. In exercises after this one, readers will decide whether an intransitivizing pronoun is needed or whether it cannot be in the sentence.

Answers will be provided after the exercises. Answers will be supplemented – when needed – with a few brief comments to contrast a sentence with and without a reflexive pronoun.

These exercises are primarily intended as sample exercises that teachers can adapt to the level and needs of their students. The answers provided will be in present tense by default. However, teachers can adapt these exercises to practice other tenses. Second language learners can certainly benefit from doing the exercises. Some of the more advanced exercises in Chapter 4 might be challenging enough for teachers and for some native speakers.

1   (Yo)/levantar/ 7:00 de la mañana. ([Yo] Me levanto a las 7:00 de la mañana)
2   (Tú)/bañar/ antes de/vestirte.

3   (Nosotros)/arreglar/antes de salir.
4   Gloria/peinar/el pelo/antes de cepillarse los dientes.
5   Maruja/peinar/antes de cepillarse los dientes.
6   Marina/cepillar/los dientes/antes de cepillar/los dientes/a la niña.
7   Los estudiantes/duchar/cada mañana.
8   (Yo)/no/afeitar/los fines de semana.
9   Rosa y yo/vestir/antes de desayunar.
10 (Tú)/desayunar/antes de cepillarse/los dientes. (The intransitivizing pronoun in *cepillarse* changes when *desayunar* is conjugated).
11 (Yo)/cambiar/la camisa diariamente.
12 Esta jugadora/llamar/Tatiana.
13 (Ella)/estirar/antes de hacer ejercicio.
14 (Ella)/preparar/bien para los partidos.
15 Después de cada partido/(ella) bañar.
16 Después de/bañar,/secar.
17 Primero/(ella) poner/la ropa interior.
18 Luego/(ella) poner/desodorante.
19 (Ella)/poner la blusa/antes de/poner los pantalones.
20 Al final, /secar el pelo/y/pintar los labios.

Exercise 2. *¿Qué hace José?* 'What is José doing?' Conjecture what José is probably doing according to the clues given. Several answers are possible. (Compare your answers with the answers given after the exercise. NOT all of the sentences require an intransitivizing pronoun).

21 Son las 7:00 de la mañana. El reloj despertador de José suena.
22 Son las 7:01 de la mañana. José se baja de la cama.
23 Son las 7:02 de la mañana. José está en la ducha.
24 Son las 7:06 de la mañana. José tiene una toalla en la mano.
25 José tiene crema de afeitar en la cara.
26 José tiene ropa en la cama y en las manos.
27 José está al frente de los zapatos.
28 José tiene una corbata en una mano.
29 José pasa por la puerta del cuarto. (Esta oración no es reflexiva).
30 José tiene una taza, cereal y leche.
31 José está en el comedor y tiene cereal, café y fruta en la mesa.
32 José está de pie. Ahora procede a acomodarse en la silla.
33 José ya no está sentado. Deja la silla.
34 José tiene un cepillo de dientes y crema dental en la mano.
35 José ya no está en la casa. Ahora abre la puerta del carro. Después de abrir la puerta del carro, José . . .

Exercise 3. Write (or say) full sentences with the information given. Now you will have to decide whether the sentence needs a reflexive pronoun or not. Answers and a few brief comments after the exercise.

36   La mamá/despertar/a la niña/a las 7:00 de la mañana.
37   La niña/despertar/a la niña/a las 7:00 de la mañana.
38   La niña/levantar/a las 7:00 de la mañana.
39   La mamá/duchar/la niña.
40   La niña/bañar/para ir a la escuela.
41   La niña/poner/los zapatos.
42   La niña/salir/para la escuela.
43   La niña/llegar/a la escuela.
44   La niña/saludar/a la profesora.
45   La niña/sentar/en una silla.
46   La niña/volver/a la casa.
47   La mamá/acostar/al niño de dos años.
48   La niña de siete años/poner/el pijama.
49   La niña/acostar/después de hacer la tarea.
50   La mamá/mirar/televisión/cuando los niños están acostados.

2.9. Answers to the exercises

Answers to exercise 1

51   (Yo)/levantar/7:00 de la mañana. *Yo levanto **a yo** a las 7:00 → (**Yo**) Me levanto a las 7:00 de la mañana. (cf. Levanto **a mis hijos** a las 7:30. **Mis hijos** se levantan a las 7:30.)

Students should observe that the subject pronoun is in parentheses because when it is known information, it is omitted close to 95% of the time. It is in the sentence when it is new information or when there is a change in reference (*mi esposa se levanta a las 6:00 de la mañana; yo me levanto a las 6:30 de la mañana*).

52   (Tú)/bañar/antes de/vestirte. (**Tú**) Te bañas antes de vestirte.
53   (Nosotros)/arreglar/antes de salir. (**Nosotros**) Nos arreglamos antes de salir.
54   Gloria/peinar/el pelo/ antes de cepillarse los dientes. Gloria se peina **el pelo** antes de cepillarse **los dientes**.
55   Maruja/peinar/antes de cepillarse los dientes. Maruja se peina antes de cepillarse **los dientes**.
56   Marina/cepillar/los dientes/antes de cepillar/los dientes/a la niña. Marina se cepilla **los dientes** antes de cepillarle **los dientes** a la niña.

57 Los estudiantes/duchar/cada mañana. **Los estudiantes** <u>se</u> duchan cada mañana.
58 (Yo) no/afeitar/los fines de semana. (**Yo**) No <u>me</u> afeito los fines de semana.
59 Rosa y yo/vestir/antes de desayunar. **Rosa y yo** <u>nos</u> vestimos antes de desayunar.
60 (Tú) desayunar/antes de cepillar/los dientes. (Tú) Desayunas antes de cepillar<u>te</u> **los dientes**. Also: (**Tú**) <u>te</u> desayunas antes de cepillarte los dientes. The use of a reflexive pronoun with a few verbs and without a difference in meaning is common in Latin America. Austin Moore (PC 2016) conjectured that the TE codes completeness. People break their fasting when they have breakfast.
61 (Yo)/cambiar la camisa/diariamente. (<u>**Yo**</u>) <u>Me</u> cambio **la camisa** diariamente.

Note: When not needed, the subject pronoun will be omitted from now on, both in the exercises/answers for this chapter and in the rest of the exercises/answers in this book.

62 Esta jugadora/llamar/Tatiana. **Esta jugadora** <u>se</u> llama Tatiana.
63 (Ella)/estirar/antes de hacer ejercicio. <u>Se</u> estira antes de hacer ejercicio.
64 (Ella)/preparar/bien para los partidos. <u>Se</u> prepara bien para los partidos.
65 (Ella) bañar/después de cada partido. <u>Se</u> baña después de cada partido.
66 Después de/bañar,/secar. Después de bañar<u>se</u>, <u>se</u> seca.
67 Primero/(ella) poner/la ropa interior. Primero <u>se</u> pone **la ropa interior**.
68 Luego/(ella) poner/desodorante. Luego <u>se</u> pone **desodorante**.
69 (Ella) poner la blusa/antes de/poner los pantalones. <u>Se</u> pone **la blusa** antes de poner<u>se</u> **los pantalones**.
70 Al final, /secar el pelo/y/pintar los labios. Al final, <u>se</u> seca **el pelo** y <u>se</u> pinta **los labios**.

Answers to exercise 2

71 Son las 7:00 de la mañana. El reloj despertador de José suena. → **José** (<u>se</u>) despierta. (cf. <u>José</u> oye **el despertador**.)
     Both *José despierta* and *José se despierta* are commonly used by native speakers.
72 Son las 7:01 de la mañana. José levantar. → **José** <u>se</u> levanta. (cf. *José levanta. But <u>José</u> levanta **la mano**. <u>José</u> mueve **la cobija**. **José** <u>se</u> mueve.)
73 Son las 7:02 de la mañana. José está en la ducha. → **José** <u>se</u> ducha.

74   Son las 7:06 de la mañana. José tiene una toalla en la mano. **José** <u>se</u> seca.
75   José tiene crema de afeitar en la cara. **José** <u>se</u> afeita.
76   José tiene ropa en la cama y en las manos. **José** <u>se</u> viste.
77   José está al frente de los zapatos. <u>José</u> <u>se</u> pone **los zapatos**.
78   José tiene una corbata en una mano. <u>José</u> <u>se</u> pone **la corbata**.
79   José pasa por la puerta del cuarto. (Esta oración no es reflexiva). José sale del cuarto.
80   José tiene una taza, cereal y leche. <u>José</u> prepara **el desayuno**.
81   José está en el comedor y tiene cereal, café y fruta en la mesa. <u>José</u> va a desayunar.
82   José está de pie. Ahora procede a acomodarse en la silla. **José** <u>se</u> sienta.
83   José ya no está sentado. Deja la silla. **José** <u>se</u> para. (**José** <u>se</u> paró). (<u>Se</u> levanta; <u>se</u> levantó).
84   José tiene un cepillo de dientes y crema dental en la mano. <u>José</u> <u>se</u> cepilla **los dientes**.
85   José ya no está en la casa. Ahora abre la puerta del carro. Después de abrir la puerta del carro, José . . . José (se) sube al carro.

Answers to exercise 3

86   La mamá/despertar/la niña/a las siete de la mañana. <u>La mamá</u> despierta **a la niña** a las siete de la mañana.
87   La niña/despertar/a las siete de la mañana. **La niña** <u>se</u> despierta a las siete de la mañana. (also: La niña despierta a las siete de la mañana).
88   La niña/levantar/a las 7:00 de la mañana. **La niña** <u>se</u> levanta a las 7:00 de la mañana. (cf. *La niña levanta a las siete de la mañana).
89   La mamá/bañar/la niña. <u>La mamá</u> baña **a la niña**.
90   La niña/bañar/para ir a la escuela. **La niña** <u>se</u> baña para ir a la escuela.
91   La niña/poner/los zapatos. <u>La niña</u> <u>se</u> pone **los zapatos**.
92   La niña/salir/para la escuela. <u>La niña</u> sale para la escuela.
93   La niña/llegar/a la escuela. <u>La niña</u> llega a la escuela.
94   La niña/saludar/a la profesora. <u>La niña</u> saluda **a la profesora**.
95   La niña/sentar/en una silla. **La niña** <u>se</u> sienta en una silla.
96   La niña/volver/a la casa. <u>La niña</u> vuelve a la casa.
97   La mamá/acostar/al niño de dos años. <u>La mamá</u> acuesta **al niño** de dos años.
98   La niña de 7 años/poner/el pijama. <u>La niña</u> de siete años <u>se</u> pone **el pijama**.
99   La niña/acostar/después de hacer la tarea. **La niña** <u>se</u> acuesta después de hacer la tarea.
100 La mamá/mirar televisión/cuando los niños están acostados. <u>La mamá</u> mira **televisión** cuando los niños están acostados.

Notes

1 *Se* stands for any reflexive pronoun, as explained after the paragraph where this note originated.

2 Throughout this book, the <u>verber</u> will be <u>underlined</u>; the **verbed** will be in **bold**; and the <u><u>verbee</u></u> (the indirect object) will be <u><u>double-underlined</u></u>.

   Specialized or key terms are written in CAPITAL LETTERS the first time they appear or when their mention is particularly relevant. Capitalized terms will be explained briefly as needed, either in the text itself or in endnotes like this one.

   Specialized terms that are very common are not explained. Thus, SUBJECT and DIRECT OBJECT are not explained, but NOMINATIVE and ACCUSA-TIVE (the specialized term for each of these two terms will be explained).

3 ACCUSATIVE: the DIRECT OBJECT in a sentence is said to be marked with the accusative case. In Greek grammar, the accusative was the case for the participant in the sentence that was "affected" (Butt 2006: 14). Contrary to a common understanding by many linguists (Beavers 2011; Hopper & Thompson 1980; among many other), affectedness is not necessary for direct objecthood. If you go to a bakery and admire a pie but do not buy it, nothing happens to the pie. Think of all the people that you might admire, like, or praise, but who do not even know who you are. In this book, the direct object is the participant that passes the verbed entailment when there is also a <u>verber</u> in the sentence. When there is no <u>verber</u> in a sentence, the **verbed** is "promoted" to subject (it might move to preverbal position and will agree with the verb). The subject of passive voice sentences and of most "reflexive" sentences is the **verbed**. The subject of sentences with two participants and a "reflexive" pronoun is the <u><u>verbee</u></u> (<u><u>Bernardo</u></u> se cortó **un dedo** 'Bernardo cut one of his fingers').

   DATIVE: the indirect object in a sentence is said to be marked with the dative case. The dative in a sentence (from the person who receives a gift) is the participant who gains something (<u><u>The Swedish Academy</u></u> gave **the Nobel Prize** <u><u>to Vargas Llosa</u></u>) or loses something (<u><u>un profesor</u></u> <u><u>me</u></u> robó **un libro de lingüística general** 'a professor stole from me **a book on general linguistics**'). Vargas Llosa gained a prize; I lost a book that someone stole from me.

   ANTECEDENT: An antecedent is a word, phrase, or clause referred to ENDO-PHORICALLY by another expression, which precedes or follows it.

   • In the following construction, *the boy* is the antecedent of *who: the boy who* pitched the game is worn out.
   • In the following construction, *a towel* is the antecedent of *one:* If you need *one,* there's *a towel* in the top drawer (SIL 2003). (The repetition comes from the original). ENDOPHORA is coreference of an expression with another expression either before it or after it. One expression provides the information necessary to interpret the other (SIL 2003).

4 Abbreviations: ACC: accusative; DAT: dative; REFL: reflexive

5 In terms of Relational Grammar, these sentences are unergative (the only partic-ipant heads a 1 arc; that is, the only participant is an agentive subject). In terms of Chomskian linguistics, an unergative sentence is an intransitive sentence with (just) an external argument (a subject that is the "doer").

6 Although Suñer (1976) and others (e.g. Gutiérrez Ordóñez 1999) argue that *se* cannot be replacing the subject (a definition of subject as [NP, S] (NP under S) assumed in Chomskian linguistics forces them to propose such a move), there is

plenty of evidence that the <u>impersonal</u> *se* is replacing a <u>person</u> (or at least an animate). As Perlmutter & Postal (1983: 106) observed, "A great many languages have impersonal passives". They go on to state that "It is thus predicted that in every language with impersonal Passives, *the class of intransitive predicates permitting impersonal Passive clauses is a subset of the class of unergative predicates*" (107). (Emphasis in the original). In terms of this proposal, unergative sentences are sentences whose only participant is the <u>verber</u>. That <u>verber</u> would be the one who dances, runs, sleeps, snores, swims, works, etc.

7   Schmitz (1966) observed that "reflexive for unplanned occurrences" can be found in Bolinger et al. (1960: 201). After chasing a copy of Bolinger's textbook for over ten years, this author finally saw a third edition (1973) a few days before this manuscript went to press. Reflexive for unplanned occurrences is explained on page 233. Thanks to Mary Friedman for giving me this copy on July 27, 2021. An electronic copy of the first edition can be found at this site: https://openlibrary.org/books/OL26690691M/Modern_Spanish

For an explanation of an UNPLANNED OCCURRENCE, as understood in the 1960s, see Bull (1965: 267), who writes, "The reflexive denies that an exterior agent is involved and, by implication, puts the responsibility on the subject. It is frequently used, as a result, to avoid accepting the responsibility for an event (*Patrón, no lo rompí, se me rompió*)". This is easily the most egregious and completely unjustified stereotype of Spanish grammar.

8   IO: indirect object

9   RÉGIMEN: In traditional Spanish grammar, a verb is said to REGIR 'govern' accusative or dative case. In simple English, that means that a verb will require (or accept) a direct object or an indirect object. The verb *belong* in English would be said to govern dative case because its single object cannot be a direct object (an object marked with the accusative case), but it governs a dative case because its only object has to be introduced by the preposition *to* (**this book** belongs <u>to you</u>).

10   ??*Estela sirvió una taza de café* seems somewhat "unground-ed". In a way, "*se parece a*" the sentence **Estela put deodorant* (as opposed to *Estela put deodorant on*). In *Estela se sirvió una taza de café* 'Estela served a cup of coffee for herself', all of the pieces are together, but they are not in ??*Estela sirvió una taza de café*. This last sentence seems to be missing a "piece" ("valence" is the specialized term in linguistics, a term adapted from chemistry by Lucien Tesnière, a French linguist who died in 1954).

11   A few scholars working on other languages have proposed that a "reflexive" pronoun replaces the subject, not the direct object. Marantz (1984: 152–156) might have been the first scholar to propose that a reflexive pronoun "absorbs" the external argument (the subject in Chomskian linguistics). It is possible that Marantz was drawing on work by Kayne (1975). Grimshaw (1990: 154) concurs with Marantz. Grimshaw works on French, a language that offers cues that the subject in reflexive sentences is not the underlying subject because the auxiliary is the equivalent of *be*, and therefore that "reflexive" pronoun must be replacing the external argument (the subject). Similar evidence is "visible" in other languages with a distinction between *have* and *be* as the auxiliary for the perfect tenses. In terms of this book, the subject of reflexive sentences is the **verbed** or the <u>verbee</u>, not the <u>verber</u>.

12   What is a participant ON THE SURFACE vs. an UNDERLYING participant? In a sentence like *We sent flowers to Grandma*, the subject, direct object, and indirect object are in the canonical place of a canonical sentence in English.

Each of those grammatical relations are in their UNDERLYING function and in their SURFACE function; the surface function being the function audible to the listener/visible to the reader. The GRAMMATICAL SUBJECT, DIRECT OBJECT, and INDIRECT OBJECT are also the LOGICAL SUBJECT, DIRECT OBJECT, AND INDIRECT OBJECT. The GRAMMATICAL subject (the subject by FORM – by position and by agreement) is the same as the LOGICAL subject (the subject by MEANING). In the variation of the sentence expressed as *Grandma was sent flowers*, *Grandma* is the surface subject (by position and by agreement), but it is the underlying indirect object; that is, the participant who received flowers and has them. Even in the variation of the sentence *We sent Grandma flowers* (the variation with primary object and secondary object, as proposed in Dryer 1986), *Grandma* is the beneficiary, and *flowers* is what was sent. Remember that verber, **verbed**, and verbee remain constant in different alternations (variations) of the same sentence. Speakers of English can say *we sent Grandma flowers* because, when unshifted, this sentence will necessarily revert to *we sent flowers to Grandma*. The flowers are **the sent**, and Grandma is the beneficiary (she has flowers). Grandma cannot be the **sent**, because if it is true that *we sent Grandma flowers*, it is not true that we sent Grandma anywhere. People send flowers to grandmothers; people do not send grandmothers to flowers. That is part of the fundamentally simple logic of language that verber, **verbed**, and verbee bring to the new understanding of language proposed in González (2021) and in this book.

References

Ávila López-Pedraza, Julio. 2009. Análisis de los usos de *se* desde la gramática descriptiva. *Hispania* 92.791–799. www.jstor.org/stable/40648461.

Beavers, John. 2011. On affectedness. *Natural Language and Linguistic Theory* 29.335–370. www.jstor.org/stable/41475292.

Bello, Andrés. [1847]1941. *Gramática de la lengua castellana*. With notes by Rufino J. Cuervo. Buenos Aires: Librería Perlado Editores.

Bolinger, Dwight L. & Turner, Ronald C. [1960]1973. *Modern Spanish. A project of the Modern Language Association*. 3rd. edn. New York: Harcourt, Brace, and Jovanovich, Inc.

Bull, William. E. [1965]1984. *Spanish for teachers. Applied linguistics*. FL: Malabar.

Butt, Miriam. 2006. *Theories of case*. New York: Cambridge University Press.

Chomsky, Noam. 1993. *Lectures on government and binding*. The Pisa Lectures. Berlin: Mouton de Gruyter.

De Benito Moreno, Carlota. 2010. Las oraciones pasivas e impersonales con *se*. Estudio sobre el ALPI. *Dialectología* 5.1–25. www.edicions.ub.edu/revistes/dialectologia5/.

Dryer, Mathew S. 1986. Primary objects, secondary objects, and antidative. *Language* 62.808–845.

García, Erica C. 1975. *The role of theory in linguistic analysis. The Spanish pronoun system*. Amsterdam: North Holland Publishing Company.

González, Luis H. 2021. *The fundamentally simple logic of language: Learning a second language with the tools of the native speaker*. London: Routledge.

Grimshaw, Jane. 1990. *Argument structure*. Cambridge, MA: The MIT Press.

Gutiérrez Ordóñez, Salvador. 1999. Los dativos. In Bosque Muñoz, Ignacio & Demonte Barreto, Violeta (eds.), *Gramática descriptiva de la lengua española*, vol. 2, 1855–1930. Madrid: Espasa Calpe.

Haspelmath, Martin. 2019. Comparing reflexive constructions in the world's languages. (Draft version of June 18, 2019). www.academia.edu/39975707/Comparing_reflex ive_constructions_in_the_worlds languages.

Hopper, Paul J. & Thompson, Sandra A. 1980. Transitivity in grammar and discourse. *Language* 56.251–295.

Huddleston, Rodney & Pullum, Geoffrey K. 2002. *The Cambridge grammar of the English language*. Cambridge: Cambridge University Press.

Jackendoff, Ray S. 1972. *Semantic interpretation in generative grammar*. Cambridge, MA: The MIT Press.

Kayne, Richard. 1975. *French syntax*. Cambridge, MA: The MIT Press.

Maldonado, Ricardo. [1999]2006. *A media voz. Problemas conceptuales del clítico se*. México, DF: Universidad Nacional Autónoma de México.

Marantz, Alec. 1984. *On the nature of grammatical relations*. Cambridge, MA: The MIT Press.

Mendikoetxea, Amaya. 1999. Construcciones con *se*: medias, pasivas e impersonales. In Bosque, Ignacio & Demonte Barreto, Violeta (eds.), *Gramática descriptiva de la lengua española*, vol. 2, 1631–1722. Madrid: Espasa Calpe S.A.

Perlmutter, David M. & Postal, Paul M. 1983. The 1-advancement exclusiveness law. In Perlmutter, David M. & Rosen, Carol G. (eds.), *Studies in relational grammar*, vol. 2, 81–125. Chicago: The University of Chicago Press.

Sánchez López, Cristina. 2002. *Las construcciones con* se. Madrid: Visor.

Schmitz, John Robert. 1966. The *se me* construction: reflexive for unplanned occurrences. *Hispania* 49(3). 430–433. https://doi.org/10.2307/337456.

SIL. 2003. *Glossary of linguistic terms*. Dallas, TX: Summer Institute of Linguistics. (Last accessed 2021). SIL (2003) was last updated in 2003. https://glossary.sil.org/.

Silverstein, Michael. 1976. Hierarchy of features and ergativity. In Dixon, R. M. W. (ed.), *Grammatical categories in Australian languages*, 112–171. Canberra: Australian Institute of Aboriginal Studies.

Suñer, Margarita. 1976. Demythologizing the impersonal "se" in Spanish. *Hispania* 59(2). 268–275. https://www.jstor.org/stable/339502.

Van Valin, Robert D. Jr. & LaPolla, Randy J. 1997. *Syntax. Structure, meaning and function*. Cambridge, UK: Cambridge University Press.

Whitley, M. Stanley. 2002. *Spanish/English contrasts. A course in Spanish linguistics*. 2nd edn. Washington, DC: Georgetown University Press.

3 How the intransitivizing *se* accounts for true reflexive *se*, but not the other way around

3.1. The view from above: against the need for the ten to 15 different functions of *se*

The traditional explanation for reflexive constructions in Spanish is based on a list of ten to 15 "functions of *se*", which have a long-standing name for structures like those in (1–11) below, but do not have a name for other structures that might not have been recognized, as Chapter 4 shows. Whitley (2002: 173–184) discussed the following functions, and he stops at 11 because those are enough for students (and scholars) to try to digest. We are going to show that all of them are clearly explained as <u>verber</u> intransitivization, without the need for the categories, and above all, without the need for explanations that complicate the issue by adding unnecessary distinctions (meaning changing/inchoative *se*, *se* of emotional reaction, unplanned or accidental *se*, etc.). No wonder students seem to give up on understanding parts of the grammar of a second language when even some teachers or scholars realize that the categories are more than any learner or scholar can handle, as observed by Whitley (2002: 184) when he writes, "the other nine are more than sufficient". Here is the list of functions of *se* in Whitley (2002: 173–184). There are 11 here. Whitley puts passive and impersonal *se* in the same category. "Spurious" *se* is omitted (an indirect object clitic *le(s)* that becomes *se* before a following pronoun beginning with l-). That *se* and the reflexive *se* are a coincidence in sound (homophony). A translation for each sentence appears after the examples.

(1) True reflexive *se* (of a direct object) **Olga** <u>se</u> vio en el espejo.[1]

(2) True reflexive (of an indirect object) <u>Olga</u> <u>se</u> compró **una blusa**.

(3) Impersonal *se* <u>Se</u> caminó todo el día.

DOI: 10.4324/9781003214090-3

(4)	Passive *se* (= **este edificio** <u>se</u> remodeló)	<u>Se</u> cierra **la puerta** a la 1:00 PM.
(5)	Causative *se*	<u>Rosa</u> <u>se</u> cortó **el pelo**; <u>Juan</u> <u>se</u> operó ayer.
(6)	"Unplanned or accidental *se*"	Al almuerzo <u>se</u> <u>nos</u> servirá(n) **butifarras**.
(7)	Intransitivizing *se*	**El aluminio** <u>se</u> ha fundido.
(8)	Reflexive *se* of emotional reaction	**Ellos** <u>se</u> aburrieron (de la tele).
(9)	Reciprocal *se*	**Ustedes** <u>se</u> casaron.
(10)	Lexical or inherent *se*	**Ella** <u>se</u> quejó de la sopa.
(11)	Meaning-changing/inchoative *se*	<u>Ella</u> <u>se</u> bebió **el café**.

The translation for each sentence is as follows: (1) Olga saw herself in the mirror. (2) Olga bought a blouse (for herself). (3) People/one walked all day. (4) Someone closes the door at 1:00 PM; the door gets closed at 1:00 PM. (5) Rosa cut her hair; Juan had surgery yesterday (he was operated on). (6) We will be served Catalan sausage at lunch. (7) The aluminum has melted. (8) They got bored (from watching TV). (9) You (two) got married. (10) She complained about the soup. (11) She drank her coffee.

Sentences (1–11) above present Whitley's functions in a slightly different order because the ordering will help in the explanation. In fact, one function often leads to the next. Chapter 2 has accounted for the first seven functions (1–7). A common problem of the functions is that they are so difficult to tell apart that professors of Spanish in college (including native speakers who are linguists) have approached me after presentations of this analysis and admitted that they themselves cannot tell apart several functions from the others. They are also put on the spot by students who ask why a function is *x* and not *y*. That comment is echoed below by Whitley (2002: 180). Observe how (4) (and for that matter 3) and (7) are undistinguishable, particularly with a <u>verber</u> intransitivization explanation. *Se cierra(n) **las puertas*** is presumably ambiguous: if the verb is in the singular form, it is an impersonal sentence (3); if in the plural form, passive *se* (4). If the **verbed** noun in the preceding example is singular (Se cierra ***la puerta***), there is no way of knowing whether the sentence is an impersonal or a passive *se*. It is possible to argue that it is an impersonal *se* sentence if *se* is the first word in the sentence, and that it is a passive *se* if the **verbed** precedes the *se* in the sentence (*<u>se</u> cerró **la puerta*** vs. *la puerta <u>se</u> cerró*). However, that difference in word order is something that only scholars might notice. It is difficult to see it in the regular use of language because speakers see only one of these two sentences at a time.[2]

The example given for "unplanned or accidental *se*" (6) is unlike the typical example for that construction in textbooks and even in scholarly accounts. The purpose was to show that (6) cannot be an accidental or unplanned *se* (as it is not a sentence like *a Vargas Llosa se le dio el Premio Nóbel*). It is the opposite: the events portrayed in those sentences are deliberate, well planned, and pondered, to state it with three verbs that come immediately to mind. By the way, we see again the possibility of impersonal (singular) or passive *se* inside (6). Not only are those categories in (1–11) unnecessary; they are confusing and therefore misleading. Sentences (12a-e) are typical examples for sentences like (6). They are commonly found in textbooks and scholarly accounts. Sentences (12f,g) are the same pattern, yet they will hardly be found in a discussion of the topic. The pattern is much more productive than previously thought. In fact, the robustness of indirect object and intransitivizing *se* in Spanish suggests that the number of sentences like (6) and (12) is infinite.

(12) a. **Tomás** <u>se</u> <u>nos</u> *murió.*
      'Thomas died on us'.
   b. **El peine** <u>se</u> <u>nos</u> *cayó.*
      'Our comb fell; we dropped our comb'.
   c. <u>Se</u> <u>les</u> *perdieron* **las llaves**.
      'They lost their keys'.
   d. <u>Se</u> <u>me</u> *rompieron* **las gafas**.
      'My glasses broke'.
   e. <u>Se</u> <u>me</u> *olvidó* **la tarea**.
      'I forgot my homework'.
   f. <u>Se</u> <u>me</u> *fue* **la paloma/la palabra**.
      'I lost my train of thought'.
   g. <u>Se</u> <u>les</u> *armó* **un lío**.
      'They got into some trouble'.

Based on the preceding examples, there is some reason to believe in a putative "unplanned or accidental happening". However, when other examples are brought to the discussion, an attentive observer will notice that the accidentality is a function (a result) of the meaning of the verb, not of the construction (intransitivizing *se* + indirect object). This point is clear when readers consider sentence (6), the Vargas Llosa sentences in (11) in §2.3, and the sentences about (**some**) *oil leaking out of a tank* or **the** *oil leaking out of a tank* in §4.3, whose explanation will be much easier to understand after sentence (11) above is explained.[3]

Let us proceed to sentences (8–11). Sentence (8) is a very productive use of *se*. It is a simple intransitivization. If *la televisión **los** aburrió **a ellos*** 'television bored **them**', then **they** got/were bored (by television). As Whitley (2002: 180) put it:

> Syntactically, this category could be analyzed either as inchoative *se* (cf. *se preocupó* vs. *está preocupado* like *se durmió* vs. *está dormido*) or as intransitivizing *se* (*él me alegró, yo me alegré,* **me alegré a mí mismo*). Babcock (1970), though, placed such verbs in their own category more because of their semantic properties as psych verbs.

(Remember that the notation "*" means a sentence that speakers never or rarely use in their normal use of language).

The fact that those verbs might have a non-human <u>verber</u> affecting a human **verbed** is not a reason to put them in a different category. Those verbs make up transitive sentences and the *se* replaces the <u>verber</u>, like in any regular transitive sentence. By the way, the reader will have realized by now that with <u>verber</u> and **verbed**, all verbs are so much more regular than we have ever thought. Including the famous verbs of "emotional reaction", which are known in linguistics as psych(ological) verbs because a human participant experiences an emotion, cognition, perception, etc. Roughly speaking, the most interesting psych verbs are those whose **verbed** is human (or at least animate) and whose subject is inanimate.

Although it is true that a reflexive pronoun sometimes expresses reciprocity (*los novios se miraron, los novios se pelearon, los novios se abrazaron*), sentence (9) is not a reciprocal sentence, contrary to what is stated in many textbooks and pedagogical grammars of Spanish (and of other languages). The *se* is there to show that the two folks who got married are the **married**, not the <u>marriers</u>. The <u>verber</u> is simply left out of the picture more often than not.[4] The marrier was a priest, a pastor, or a judge. I can say that *yo caso* 'I marry', only if I am a priest, a pastor, or a judge. Even a pastor or a judge who is getting married will have to be married to their loved one by another pastor or judge.

There are legitimate uses of a reciprocal intransitivizing pronoun. But reciprocal sentences should get a new look to distinguish what is really reciprocal in meaning and what is simply <u>verber</u> intransitivization. Observe these two very interesting contrasts. First, *mis dos hermanas A y B no hablan* vs. *mis dos hermanas A y B no se hablan* 'My two sisters A and B do not speak (cannot speak) vs. my two sisters A and B do not speak to each other'. This last sentence is reciprocal. On the other hand, is a sentence like *Marina y Orlando se casaron el mismo día* 'Marina and Orlando married the same day' reciprocal, as explained for similar sentences in several textbooks? The answer is "not necessarily". Marina and Orlando could be a sister and a brother who each married someone else, yet Spanish speakers would have to use an intransitivizing ("reciprocal") *se* to express that state of affairs. The *se* is required to indicate that both of them are the married, not the marrier, regardless of whether they are a couple, and were married (by a priest, pastor, or judge) to each other, or whether they are a sister and a brother who were each married to a different person. *Se casaron* simply means 'got married' (i.e., they are the married, not the marrier), because not even a pastor or judge can officiate their own wedding. Actually, the phrase *el mismo día* 'the same day' suggests that they might not be husband and wife. Notice also the contribution of world knowledge to the interpretation of that sentence. Those familiar with Orlando and Marina will know that they are brother and sister and that the sentence is referring to them getting married with another person each.

To summarize, some uses of the so-called reciprocal pronoun are simply verber intransitivization, which has been overblown to an interpretation that is clearly incorrect, because the infamous functions of *se* have been multiplied unnecessarily. In fact, a reciprocal interpretation is possible with some verbs, but that meaning is likely more a result of the meaning of the verb than a result of the "reciprocal" pronoun. Indeed, a true reflexivization is often distinguished from a "reciprocal" interpretation by adding "mutually" or "one to the other", respectively. Thus, the reciprocity is more in the "one to the other" (and conversely), than in the intransitivizing *se*.

Sentence (10) is an inherently reflexive sentence. There are a few verbs in Spanish (and presumably in many languages) that are always used with a reflexive pronoun, and at least some of them started as transitive verbs.[5] The prototypical reflexive might be *suicidarse* 'commit suicide', which is in Latin self-kill).[6] Some fairly common ones (and some more frequent than *suicidarse*) are *darse cuenta de* 'realize', *atreverse* 'dare', *arrepentirse*

Table 3.1 Frequency of ten inherently reflexive verbs. Data from year 2018 (Ngram Viewer, accessed in 2021)

Se dio cuenta (de)	0.0029284494%
Se atrevió (a)	0.0007723381%
Se quejó (de)	0.0005616998%
Se arrepintió (de)	0.0002020461%
Se escapó (de)	0.0001736838%
Se suicidó	0.0001507149%
Se abstuvo (de)	0.0000818129%
Se ausentó	0.0000316704%
Se jactó (de)	0.0000292438%
Se atuvo (a)	0.0000115702%

'repent', *escaparse* 'escape', *abstenerse* 'abstain', *jactarse* 'boast', *atenerse* 'abide by', *ausentarse* 'absent oneself', *quejarse* 'complain'. Table 3.1 with data from Ngram Viewer (2021) shows the relative frequency of ten of these verbs. The search was done in July 2021.

Atrever and *jactar* were transitive in Latin and in old Spanish (Bello [1847] 1941: 200), but they evolved to the point of mandatory reflexivization. Whitley (2002: 177) reports that Roldán (1971) noted that inherently reflexive verbs also pass the *estar* + *participle* test that inchoatives and "meaning changing verbs" pass: *se enojó*, then *está enojada*; *se arrepintió*, then *está arrepentida*. This observation shows again the difficulty of keeping apart the functions. Furthermore, it provides additional evidence for the meaning of *se*. If *se* indicates that the subject is the **verbed**, then if *X* repented (*X se arrepintió*), then *X is repented* (*X es la arrepentida* because *X está arrepentida*). Thus, inherently reflexive verbs are consistent with the meaning of *se* as <u>verber</u> omission, mandatory in this case. In fact, most of the inherently reflexive verbs are transparent: the only participant in the sentence is the **verbed**, as <u>verber</u> intransitivization predicts. A deeper look at inherent reflexives is another issue for further research.[7] In a way, this is mandatory reflexivization, as when one dresses herself or himself or puts on or takes off a hat, including tipping off one's hat to someone else (*Me <u>le</u> quito **el sombrero** al difunto Ivan Sag* 'I take my hat off to the late Ivan Sag', for example). The reader is invited to see why the <u>me</u> is there. I trust that readers will figure it out. It might take some thinking. As I tell my students, grammar (learning, in general) is like an old mine: you have to dig deep. Here is the answer. If (<u>yo</u>) <u>le</u> quito **el sombrero** a <u>Ivan Sag</u>, I am removing his hat; however, if (<u>yo</u>) <u>me</u> <u>le</u> quito **el sombrero** a <u>Ivan Sag</u>, I am taking off my own hat to show respect to him. Observe that the sentence in Spanish has two indirect objects. But that is a tangent not to pursue here.

3.2. You can *drink up your coffee* but you cannot *drink up coffee

I have saved (11) for last because it is perhaps the hardest distinction to understand, and it has been carrying a heavy weight, at least since 1847, when Bello ([1847]1941: 199) wrote that affectedness, intention ('conato'), good disposition, etc. was the difference between drinking two *azumbres* 'liters' of wine instead of drinking wine. Let Whitley (2002: 176) summarize our understanding of this contrast:

> The verbs of this category (1) contrast with nonreflexive versions (unlike lexical reflexives), (2) fail the *a sí mismo test* for true reflexivity

(**ella se bebió el café a sí misma*), and (3) show a special shift of meaning. In *reírse, olvidarse, temerse, entrarse, merecerse, beberse, comerse, se* intensifies the action like the English particles *up, down, out, away* (v. 10.5). For Bello ([1847] 1958: 246) and Ramsey ([1894] 1956: 380), what is intensified is the involvement or affect of the Subj as simultaneous IO. Bello's glossings are illustrative:

> *me temo*: 'el interés de la persona que habla'
> *se lo bebió*: 'la buena disposición, el apetito, la decidida voluntad'
> *te los sabes*: 'la presunción de saberlo todo'
> *te entraste*: 'cierto conato o fuerza con que se vence algún estorbo'

There is no change in meaning, as will be shown below. The difference is ASPECTUAL (referring to the beginning, middle, or end of an event or state). See Table 3.2 below. Nor is there any need to invoke affectedness, heightened interest, good disposition, appetite, conscious will ('decidida voluntad'), etc., as Bello (1941[1847]: 199) wrote, and as many scholars have mindlessly repeated for over 170 years. Consider that a patient who swallows a disgusting medicine might not have a willful, gusto-like attitude or disposition to drink something unappetizing, but the patient knows that they have to get to the bottom of the dose as the following sentence makes clear:

(13)   The patient drank the medicine down, but made an awful face.

Let us explain *drinking coffee* vs. *drinking (up/down) the coffee* (a cup of coffee, the coffee that was served, or all the coffee available to drink at the moment) the same way we explained *putting deodorant on*, after looking at the following table, which will be briefly explained after the examples.

Table 3.2 Aktionsart classes (from Van Valin & LaPolla 1997: 93, example 3.12)[8]

State *be, have, believe*	+static	-telic	-punctual
Activity *cry, eat, run, snore*	-static	-telic	-punctual
Accomplishment *learn, melt, redden*	-static	+telic	-punctual
Achievement *break, pop, see*	-static	+telic	+punctual

(14) a. *Estela bebió* **café**.
          'Estela drank (some) coffee'.
      b. *Estela le bebió **el café** a Estela.
          (Hypothetical sentence that has to reflexivize)
      c. *Estela se bebió **el café**.
          Estela REFL drank the coffee
          'Estela drank up (down) her coffee'.
      d. *Estela se bebió **café**.
          Estela REFL drank coffee
      e. ??Estela bebió **el café**.

Remember that the notation "??" means a marginal sentence (Maldonado [1999]2006: 43). This author does not remember hearing sentences like (14e).

Let us turn to Table 3.2. Activities are not static, which means that they are dynamic (actions); they are ATELIC, which means that they are not necessarily complete; and they are not punctual, which means that they have some duration (they are not point-like; they take more than one or two seconds to be completed). ACCOMPLISHMENTS are actions, they are complete, and they are durative; that is, they take a clear interval of time to be completed. ACHIEVEMENTS are like accomplishments, but they are not durative, which means that they are completed in seconds, or even in a fraction of a second. *Estela drank coffee* in (14a) is an activity. That means that she drank an indefinite amount of coffee: a sip of coffee, or several sips of coffee, or several cups of coffee. On the other hand, *Estela drank her coffee* is an accomplishment. That means that we are referring to an event that is complete. In that case, it will be expressed in Spanish as *Estela se bebió el café*. That is simply TELICITY (i.e. completeness). Crucially, it is not necessarily emphasis. *Estela se bebió el café* means that she drank all of the coffee that was served to her or all of the coffee that was available. Either of those two interpretations indicates telicity (completeness), as opposed to the atelicity or incompleteness of (14a). That is the relevant difference between sentences like (14a) and (14c). Interestingly, there is a clear correlation in Spanish (and presumably in many other languages) between the presence of the intransitivizing *se* and the definite article. The combination of the two gives as a result the interpretation of totality. Sentence (14d) is clearly ungrammatical because an accomplishment interpretation clashes semantically with the activity interpretation implied by the absence of the definite article (___ *café*). Sentence (14e) is presumably acceptable to just a few native speakers.

Notice that *se tomó café* is a sound sentence; it is an "impersonal *se*" (someone/some people drank some coffee). Interestingly, *tomó el café* (without *se*) means that the person grabbed the coffee, not that the person drank it. Readers familiar with Spanish know that *to drink* is 'beber' and 'tomar'. The most common meaning of *tomar* is also 'take'.

The meaning component of *emphasis*, a common explanation offered for this contrast, is not correct. Emphasis does not necessarily lead to completion. On the other hand, completion might be achieved without the putative emphasis that has been incorrectly associated with this structure. Drinking the whole dose of a disgusting medicine does not require emphasis but it results in completeness. A putative "meaning change" (due to *se*) is an explanation that cannot be maintained after Vendler (1957) Aktionsart distinctions. The difference at work is activity vs. accomplishment or achievement. End of story. Now readers will understand the more difficult contrast in (15a-b), to which I have added (15c-e) to bring to the discussion other factors that will help the reader see a better picture:

(15) a. *Los niños durmieron diez horas.*
   'The children slept for ten hours'.
   b. *Los niños se durmieron diez horas.
   The children REFL slept for ten hours.[9]
   *'The children fell asleep for ten hours'.
   c. *El paseo en el coche durmió **a los niños**.*
   The ride in the car slept the children-ACC
   'The car ride made the children fall asleep'.
   d. *El paseo en el coche se durmió a los niños.
   The car ride REFL slept the children
   '*The car ride fell asleep the children'.
   e. **Los niños** <u>se</u> *durmieron.*
   The children REFL slept
   'The children fell asleep'.

Sentence (15a) is an activity (an interesting one, to be sure; I did not want to shy away from a common but challenging example). In fact, when people sleep, they keep breathing; in a sense, they are doing something to stay alive. The *se* in (15e) indicates that the children are the *dormidos* (i.e. they are sleeping); that is, they are asleep because they fell asleep. If we can find a plausible <u>verber</u>, all of the facts will fall into place. If we took the children for a car ride, as in (15c) (something that my wife and I actually did a few times to make them fall asleep), that is a bona fide <u>verber</u>. People fall asleep all the time because tiredness causes them to become sleepy until they fall asleep. The difference is again activity vs. accomplishment. Sentence (15b) is ungrammatical because falling asleep is an achievement, which is punctual, and cannot last ten hours. Sentence (15d) is also ungrammatical because the <u>verber</u> and the <u>se</u> cannot both appear in the same sentence.

Those are the 11 sentences with a reflexive pronoun (1–11) discussed in Whitley (2002: 173–184), and all of them were explained with <u>verber</u> intransitivization, without the need to invoke types of sentences, types of verbs, categories, etc. There was no need for further analytical tests, because the only tools needed are the <u>verber</u> entailment and the **verbed** entailment. Those two entailments are already part of grammar, as proposed in González (2021).

3.3. Conclusions

This chapter has shown that if an intransitivizing pronoun is replacing the <u>verber</u>, then the new grammatical subject is the **verbed**. Readers will remember that if there is a <u>verber</u> in the sentence, it is always the subject. When there is no <u>verber</u> in a sentence, the **verbed** is "promoted" to subject (as predicted by the Verber/Verbed Argument Selection Principle in Chapter 1). The rule that the **verbed** is promoted to subject when there is no <u>verber</u> in a sentence explains passive voice and all of the sentences in (1–11). Since Chapter 2 explained sentences (1–7), this chapter focuses on sentences (8–11). A sentence like *la tele **los** aburrió* 'TV bored **them**' is intransitivized as (**ellos**) *se aburrieron de la tele* 'they got bored from watching TV' the same way any transitive sentence is. Most psych(ological) verbs (verbs of emotional reaction) are transitive (González 2021: §3.4); therefore, they can intransitivize with *se*, and they do. Although there are "truly" reciprocal sentences, some of those sentences are better explained as <u>verber</u> intransitivization. Two people who get married *se casan* in Spanish (they do not *casan*). The mandatory intransitivizing pronoun indicates that they are the **married**, not the <u>marriers</u>. Inherently reflexive verbs have <u>verber</u> and **verbed**, and only one of them is expressed; the other is replaced with the intransitivizing pronoun. The resulting sentence passes the entailments of a **verbed**: if *Jennifer se ausentó* 'Jennifer absented' (cf. *Jennifer ausentó), then *Jennifer está ausente* (i.e. she is absent; she is not here). Finally, if *Estela bebió **café*** 'Estela drank **coffee**', then coffee was drunk (and that sentence expresses an activity); if *Estela se bebió el café* 'Estela drank her coffee', then THE coffee was drunk. The *se* and the *el* 'the' code the completeness of an accomplishment, as opposed to the activity reading in drinking coffee (cf. drinking your [the] coffee, an accomplishment). An explanation based on activities vs. accomplishments cannot be used in the L2 classroom; however, the same explanation in terms of part and whole can: *Estela bebió café* 'Estela drank (some) coffee' expresses part; *Estela* *se bebió el café* 'Estela drank her coffee' indicates that she drank all of her serving; that is, her whole serving.

3.4. Exercises

Intransitivize each sentence by replacing the <u>verber</u> with the corresponding intransitivizing pronoun.

Note: These exercises are primarily intended to be sample exercises that teachers can adapt to the level and needs of their students. The answers provided will be in present tense by default. However, teachers can adapt these exercises to practice any tense. Second language learners can certainly benefit from doing the exercises. Some of the more advanced exercises in Chapter 4 might be challenging enough for teachers and for some native speakers.

1   <u>El portero</u> abre **las puertas** a las 6:00 de la mañana.
2   <u>Una empleada</u> lee **los pedidos que se han hecho por el Internet.**
3   <u>Un empleado</u> prepara **el café**.
4   <u>La gerente</u> reúne **a los jefes de sección**.
5   <u>Un cliente</u> hace **un pedido muy grande**.
6   <u>El pedido</u> alegra mucho **a la gerente de ventas**.
7   <u>Los empleados</u> procesan **el pedido**.
8   <u>La compañía</u> envía **el pedido** por correo regular.
9   <u>El correo</u> entrega **el pedido** a tiempo.
10   <u>El cliente</u> no hace **los pagos** a tiempo.
11   <u>La compañía</u> envía **a un negociador** a hablar con el cliente.
12   <u>El negociador y el cliente</u> logran **un acuerdo**.
13   <u>El cliente</u> pide **un préstamo** en un banco.
14   <u>El banco</u> transfiere **el dinero**.
15   <u>El cliente</u> paga **el préstamo**.
16   <u>El cliente</u> recupera **la credibilidad de la empresa**.
17   <u>Los estudiantes</u> trabajan muy duro en esta Universidad.
18   <u>La cafetería</u> ofrece **distintos planes de comida**.
19   **La biblioteca** abre 16 horas al día.
20   <u>Los estudiantes</u> usan mucho **la biblioteca**.
21   <u>El despertador</u> despierta **a Margarita** a las 7:00.
22   *<u>Margarita</u> <u>le</u> peina **el pelo** <u>a Margarita</u>.
23   *<u>Margarita</u> <u>le</u> prepara **el desayuno** <u>a Margarita</u>.
24   *<u>Margarita</u> no <u>le</u> come **el pan** <u>a Margarita</u>. No está bueno.
25   <u>El Dr. Fingercut</u> operó **al tío Jorge** la semana pasada.
26   <u>El Dr. Fingercut</u> <u>le</u> hizo **una cirugía** <u>al tío Jorge</u> la semana pasada.

27   *El tío Jorge* no cuida **al tío Jorge** muy bien.
28   La medicina para calmar el dolor durmió **al tío Jorge**.
29   Este ejercicio no **nos** cansó demasiado **a nosotros**.
30   Completamos **este ejercicio** en 15 minutos.

3.5. Answers to the exercises

31   El portero abre las puertas a las 6:00 de la mañana. → **Las puertas** se abren a las 6:00 de la mañana. (Also: las puertas abren a las 6:00 de la mañana.)
32   Una empleada lee los pedidos que se han hecho por el Internet. → Se lee/se leen **los pedidos que se han hecho por el Internet**.
33   Un empleado prepara el café. → Se prepara **el café**.
34   La gerente reúne a los jefes de sección. → **Los jefes de sección** se reúnen.
35   Un cliente hizo un pedido muy grande. → Se hizo **un pedido muy grande**.
36   El pedido alegra mucho a la gerente de ventas. → **La gerente de ventas** se alegra mucho.
37   Los empleados procesan el pedido. → Se procesa **el pedido**.
38   La compañía envía el pedido por correo regular. → **El pedido** se envía por correo regular.
39   El correo entrega el pedido a tiempo. → **El pedido** se entrega a tiempo.
40   El cliente no hace los pagos a tiempo. → No se hacen **los pagos** a tiempo. (Also: no se hace **los pagos** a tiempo).
41   La compañía envía a un negociador a hablar con el cliente. → Se envía **a un negociador** a hablar con el cliente.
42   El negociador y el cliente logran un acuerdo. → Se logra **un acuerdo**.
43   El cliente pide un préstamo en un banco. → Se pide **un préstamo** en un banco.
44   El banco transfiere el dinero. → Se transfiere **el dinero**.
45   El cliente paga el préstamo. → Se paga **el préstamo**.
46   El cliente recupera la credibilidad de la empresa. → Se recupera **la credibilidad de la empresa**.
47   Los estudiantes trabajan muy duro en esta Universidad. → Se trabaja muy duro en esta universidad.
48   La cafetería ofrece distintos planes de comida. → Se ofrece/se ofrecen **distintos planes de comida**.
49   La biblioteca abre 16 horas al día. → Se abre 16 horas al día. (i.e. Se abre **la biblioteca**.)
50   Los estudiantes usan mucho la biblioteca. → **La biblioteca** se usa mucho.
51   El despertador despierta a Margarita a las 7:00. → **Margarita** se despierta a las 7:00 de la mañana.

52   *Margarita le peina el pelo a Margarita. → <u>Margarita</u> <u>se</u> peina **el pelo**.
53   *Margarita le prepara el desayuno a Margarita. → <u>Margarita</u> <u>se</u> prepara
     el desayuno.
54   *Margarita no le come el pan a Margarita. No está bueno. → <u>Margarita</u>
     no <u>se</u> come **el pan**. No está bueno.
55   El Dr. Fingercut operó al tío Jorge la semana pasada. →**El tío Jorge** <u>se</u>
     operó la semana pasada. (Also: La semana pasada <u>se</u> operó **al tío Jorge**.)
56   El Dr. Fingercut le hizo una cirugía al tío Jorge la semana pasada. → <u>El</u>
     <u>tío Jorge</u> <u>se</u> hizo **una cirugía** la semana pasada. (Also: <u>Al tío Jorge</u> <u>se</u>
     <u>le</u> hizo **una cirugía** la semana pasada.)
57   *El tío Jorge no cuida al tío Jorge muy bien. → **El tío Jorge** no <u>se</u> cuida
     muy bien.
58   La medicina para calmar el dolor durmió al tío Jorge. → **El tío Jorge**
     <u>se</u> durmió.
59   <u>Este ejercicio</u> no **nos** cansó **a nosotros**. → **(Nosotros)** No <u>nos</u> cansa-
     mos haciendo este ejercicio. (Also: Nosotros no nos cansamos con este
     ejercicio.)
60   Nosotros completamos este ejercicio en 15 minutos. → **Este ejercicio**
     <u>se</u> completó en 15 minutos.

Notes

1   Remember that throughout this book, the <u>verber</u> is underlined, the **verbed** is in
    bold, and the <u>verbee</u> is double-underlined.
    Specialized or key terms are written in CAPITAL LETTERS the first time they
    appear or when their mention is particularly relevant. Capitalized terms will be
    explained briefly as needed, either in the text itself or in endnotes like this one.
2   One of this author's students (Stephanie Keys, AKA Stephanie Simpson)
    observed approximately 15 years ago that an animate verbed tends to precede
    the *se* (**los niños** <u>se</u> bañaron 'the children bathed themselves'; 'the children were
    bathed') and that an inanimate **verbed** tends to follow (<u>se</u> abrieron **las puertas**).
    Cf. ??*el pasaporte se saca* vs. <u>se</u> saca **el pasaporte**. That is an excellent observa-
    tion that this author has quoted since then. This is an opportunity to invite readers
    or scholars to explore this issue further.
3   Marantz (1984: 141) discusses similar examples with a similar explanation for Japa-
    nese. Two of his glosses in English are 'Her son died, and Hanako was adversely
    affected' and 'It rained, and John was adversely affected' (or 'It rained on John').
4   *Ustedes casaron* is a highly unlikely sentence in Spanish. It is irrelevant for most
    purposes. It would mean something like "you officiated one/several wedding
    ceremonies".
5   English, a language with very little reflexivization, has at least three mandatory
    reflexives: avail (oneself), perjure (oneself), and pride (oneself), as observed by
    Whitley (2002: 176). The verb *absent* might be a fourth one. It is conceivable that
    there are a few other inherently reflexive verbs in English.
6   Thanks to Charlie Rowe (PC 1997) for bringing this observation to my attention.

7 The day before this manuscript was going to press, Alexandra Blum (a former student, who was kind enough to read the final version), asked this author about the *quejador* and the *quejado* in sentences with *quejarse* 'complain'. This author was glad he had written, "*most* of the inherently reflexive verbs are transparent". That wording leaves room for other verbs that might be a little too abstract. *Quejarse* 'complain' is one of them. This author had no answer for the question at the time. It is not the first time that Alexandra Blum had stumped this author. I like that!

8 These Aktionsart classes were proposed in Vendler (1957).

9 Abbreviations: ACC: accusative; REFL: reflexive pronoun

References

Babcock, Sandra. 1970. *The syntax of Spanish reflexive verbs*. The Hague: Mouton.

Bello, Andrés. [1847]1941. *Gramática de la lengua castellana*. With notes by Rufino J. Cuervo. Buenos Aires: Librería Perlado Editores.

García, Erica C. 1975. *The role of theory in linguistic analysis. The Spanish pronoun system*. Amsterdam: North Holland Publishing Company.

González, Luis H. 2021. *The fundamentally simple logic of language: Learning a second language with the tools of the native speaker*. London: Routledge.

Maldonado, Ricardo. [1999]2006. *A media voz. Problemas conceptuales del clítico* se. México, DF: Universidad Nacional Autónoma de México.

Marantz, Alec. 1984. *On the nature of grammatical relations*. Cambridge, MA: MIT Press.

Ngram Viewer. 2021. Google books ngram viewer. http://books.google.com/ngrams.

Ramsey, Marathon. [1894]1956. *A textbook of modern Spanish*. New York: Holt, Rinehart and Winston. (Revised by Robert Spaulding).

Roldán, Mercedes. 1971. Spanish constructions with *se. Language Sciences* 18.15–29.

Van Valin, Robert D. Jr. & LaPolla, Randy J. 1997. *Syntax. Structure, meaning and function*. Cambridge, UK: Cambridge University Press.

Vendler, Zeno. 1957. *Linguistics in philosophy*. Ithaca: Cornell University Press.

Whitley, M. Stanley. 2002. *Spanish/English contrasts. A course in Spanish linguistics*. 2nd edn. Washington, DC: Georgetown University Press.

4 Other "functions" of *se*

Can telling your name in another language be an idiom?

4.1. On *gone*, goer, goner, *fallen*, *dead*

We will now explain other "values" of *se*, or some sentences that will be a problem for an explanation based on the "values" or "functions" of *se*. There is a name for (and an extensive literature on) the 11 or so functions of *se* discussed in Chapter 3. As we have seen, they can all be explained as <u>verber</u> intransitivization. There might be, of course, a few details to work out, but the learning burden on students of Spanish (second language learners and even native speakers) can be reduced by at least 80%. In fact, if we are reducing ten or 11 types of sentences to one rule, we are simplifying by about ten times, just in sheer number. Let us consider a few contrasts not clearly explained, or that are proposed as yet another category. This author has never seen an explanation, other than a mere translation, for sentences like (1b):

(1) a. **Rosa fue.*
         *Rose went.
     b. ***Rosa se fue.***[1]
         Rosa REFL went
         'Rose went away'.

What makes (1b) grammatical? If the reflexive pronoun (*se*) means that the only participant in the sentence is the **verbed**, our explanation accounts for this sentence without the need to scream "idiom!" (as we, as teachers, sometimes scream when we do not know an explanation – or when there is none). It is uncontroversial that if *Rosa se fue*, she is the gone. She is gone. This is, in fact, very similar to the way (2b) works in English:

(2) a. *Rose went.
     b. Rose went away.

DOI: 10.4324/9781003214090-4

What does *Rose went away* mean? Rose is gone. That is exactly the meaning contributed by *away*. No need for any other conjectures. English, then, resembles Spanish. *Rosa se fue* is a clear achievement (a complete and instant-like event) in the sense that she went through the door's threshold and she is beyond it. She is out of here. Interestingly, not only is she the gone; she is also the goer, as English has hinted at us with the noun *goner*: gone and goer. When someone says that the mail arrived, the mail is the arrived, because the mail neither comes nor arrives by itself, really. The mail arrives when the mailperson brings it. But if we think of it, the mailperson is the arriver and the arrived. See the discussion of sentences (2a,b) in §5.1.

Let us consider a few examples with *fall* and *die*, two prototypical VER-BERLESS verbs.[2] Sentences with those verbs are called unaccusative sentences because they do not have a <u>verber</u>. The accusative (the direct object) has to unaccusativize and that **verbed** is the subject. Those sentences are verberless but not subjectless. The Verber/Verbed Argument Selection Principle (VVASP) in González (2021: Chapter 1) accounts for unaccusative verbs without the need for any modification.

(3) a. Anoche no cayó **nieve**.
     Last night no fell snow.
     'It didn't snow last night'. (No snow fell last night.)
  b. *Anoche no cayó la nieve.
     Last night no fell the snow.
  c. Anoche <u>se</u> cayó al suelo **la nieve** que había en el techo.
     Last night REFL fell to the ground the snow that was on the roof
     'The snow that was on the roof fell to the ground last night'.

As different at first sight as it might seem, the contrast in (3a) and (3c) is the same as that between *beber café* 'drink coffee' vs. *beberse el café* 'drink (up) your coffee'. The first one is an activity (atelic, i.e. incomplete), but the second is an accomplishment. The *se* and the *el* (the definite article) code totality (completeness). Notice that English codes the possession implied in the intransitivization of a sentence with an indirect object in Spanish (in sentences similar to 14c in §3.2) by using **her** *coffee* instead of **the** *coffee*. Consider also this contrast with *caer(se)*:

(4) a. *Cayó **el dictador***.
     Fell the dictator
     'The dictator fell (from power)'.
  b. ***El dictador** <u>se</u> cayó*.
     the dictator REFL fell
     'The dictator fell down'.

Caer is often accompanied by a *se*, perhaps to highlight the fact that it is an achievement (an event that is complete and point-like). One cannot *half fall* (or *half die*, for that matter). It appears that *caer* without *se* often codes a different kind of fall, for example that of a dictator or an elected official falling from power. The default meaning of *caerse* typically portrays an event of hitting the ground in a matter of seconds (or a fraction of a second). Falling from power is clearly a more durative event, lasting days, weeks, months, and even years. Interestingly, Spanish also uses *caer* (not *caerse*) when someone sinned ([*yo*] *caí* 'I sinned') or when someone fell for a joke. The absence of the reflexive pronoun is perhaps a clue that those two kinds of falling are not the prototypical act of falling.

By the same token, *morir* contrasts with *morirse*. If a person dies, the person is dead. Half-dying is a figure of speech. In Spanish, *morirse* is a common choice when people die from natural causes, including age and illness. The *se* codes the completeness of death. *Morir* is reserved for death in war, shootouts, bombings, explosions, hurricanes, and the like; that is, in criminal acts, in war, accidents, or natural disasters. In Spanish, soldiers who lose their lives in battle *mueren*, not *se mueren*. By contrast, a soldier who dies from an illness clearly not connected to combat during deployment *se murió*. In a few words, *morir* is dying (often suddenly) in criminal acts, accidents, disasters, or war, but *morirse* is what happens when people pass away due to natural causes, including illness. Here is a pair of sentences that might help readers see the difference. Observe the optionality of *se* in (5a); on the other hand, the presence of *se* is ungrammatical in (5c).

(5) a. **El Presidente** *(se) murió de neumonía.*
       the president (REFL-pronoun) died from pneumonia
       'The President died from pneumonia'.
   b. **El Presidente** *murió en un golpe de estado.*
       'The President died in a coup d'état'.
   c. *****El Presidente** se murió en un golpe de estado.

If *se* indicates that the subject is the **verbed**, and since we know that events of *falling* and *dying* are typically telic, this analysis predicts that *x fell* and *x died* should accept the presence of a reflexive pronoun with the prototypical uses of these verbs in Spanish. That prediction is borne out. *El abuelo se cayó* is more frequent than *el abuelo cayó*.[3] Notice that snow falls, and we simply refer to the fallen snow, for example. However, if I fall, I can be thought of as the faller and the fallen, unless someone tripped me, in which case we might think that I am simply the fallen. It is uncontroversial that an inanimate (like the mail, a package, a bill) is the arrived; however, the mail person is the arriver and the arrived. That is an issue for further research.

4.2. Can telling your name in another language be an idiom?

Consider telling someone's name in Spanish and in English:

(6) a. *Me llamo Alice.*
　　 b. My name is Alice.
　　 c. *La profesora se llama Alice.*
　　 d. The professor's name is Alice.

Observe that if one thinks about (6), telling your name in the other language can be called an idiom. Spanish has an intransitivizing pronoun (*me*), a verb (*llamo*), and the name (*Alice*). English has a possessive adjective (*my*), a noun (*name*), the verb *be*, and the name (*Alice*). Nothing matches, except for the name. Telling your name from one of these languages to the other is not called an idiom perhaps because telling your name is such a basic function in language. But as a linguist and professor of Spanish, I will say that if there are idioms in Spanish, this is one of them. That is, if we do not understand and produce language using <u>verber</u> and **verbed**.

Let us see how <u>verber</u> and **verbed** help understand why telling your name in many languages is different from the way English does it. More importantly, the sentence in Spanish is part of a very productive pattern: the intransitivizing pronoun in telling your name in Spanish indicates that the person is the **called**, the rule of <u>verber</u> intransitivization that accounts for virtually all of the sentences with an intransitivizing pronoun in Spanish. Consider (7), a very infrequent sentence compared with (6a,c):

(7) *<u>La mamá</u> llamó (nombró) **a la profesora** "Alice".*
　　 Her mother called (named) to the professor "Alice"
　　 '<u>Her mother</u> named **the professor** Alice'.

If anyone has to determine who is the <u>caller</u> and who is the **called** in (7), it is uncontroversial that *<u>la mamá</u>* is <u>the caller</u> and **la profesora** is **the called**. In fact, if (7) is true, (8a,b) are true, but (8c,d) are not:

(8) a. <u>La mamá</u> is the caller.　　　　 (The <u>verber</u> entailment)
　　 b. **La profesora** is the **called**.　　 (The **verbed** entailment)
　　 c. #<u>La mamá</u> is the **called**.　　　 (8c is not true if 7 is true)
　　 d. #**La profesora** is the <u>caller</u>.　 (8d is not true if 7 is true)

Observe that the <u>verber</u> in (9a,c,e,g) can be omitted, as in (9b,d,f,h), if the corresponding intransitivizing pronoun (*ME, TE, SE, NOS, OS*) replaces it. The intransitivizing pronoun shows that the only participant left in each sentence is the **verbed**.

(9) a. *La mamá llamó a la profesora Alice.*
     'Her Mom called the professor Alice'.
   b. *La profesora SE llama Alice.*
     '**The professor's** name is Alice'. (Lit: The professor is called Alice.)
   c. *Los autores llaman a este libro ¡Despierta!*
     'The authors call **this book** *Wake up!*'
   d. *Este libro SE llama ¡Despierta!*
     This book is called *Wake up!*
   e. *En español, la gente dice hola para expresar 'hello'.*
     'In Spanish, people say **hola** to express "hello"'.
   f. *En español SE dice hola para expresar 'hello'.*
     In Spanish, **hola** is said to express "hello"'.
   g. *¿Cómo dice la gente 'hello' en español?*
     'How do people say "**hello**" in Spanish?'
   h. *¿Cómo SE dice "hello" en español?*
     'How is *hello* said in Spanish?'

Although some of these sentences can be expressed in Spanish with the passive voice (the literal translation in 9b,d,f back into Spanish), Spanish overwhelmingly prefers a sentence with an intransitivizing pronoun (*este continente se llama América* 'this continent's name is America') instead of the equivalent sentence in the passive voice (??*este continente es llamado América*). Native speakers very rarely say the last sentence. This is not the place for a detailed comparison of passive with *ser* (passive voice) vs. passive with *se*, but let us show with just two examples why a passive with *se* is preferred or mandatory sometimes. (See Whitley & González 2016: 388–389, among many others, for a discussion on why in Spanish *no se usa mucho la voz pasiva* 'passive voice is not widely used').

Remember that the notation "??" means a marginal case, as proposed in Maldonado ([1999]2006: 43).

(10) a. *Ayer se oyó una explosión cerca de mi casa.*
     'Yesterday, an explosion was heard near my house'.
    b. ??Ayer fue oída **una explosión** cerca de mi casa.
     (Same as 10a)

Sentence (10a) is a passive with *se*. Sentence (10b) is a passive with *ser* 'be' (a "true" passive voice sentence). The explanation for the observation that almost no native speaker of Spanish utters sentences similar to (10b)

Table 4.1 Frequency of passive with *ser* and passive with *se* with *oír* 'hear' and *publicar* 'publish' in Ngram Viewer (2019)

Fue oída	0.0000062920%
Fue oído	0.0000072465%
Se oyó	0.0005919556%
Fue publicada	0.0001048160%
Fue publicado	0.0001408208%
Se publicó	0.0004524724%

is the fact that the verb *oír* 'hear' is low in kinesis. On the other hand, *este libro fue publicado en el año 2022* 'this book was published in the year 2022' is a good passive sentence in Spanish because *publicar* 'publish' is a verb high in kinesis. This point will make more sense to readers from languages with a robust intransitivizing pronoun, like Spanish is. Table 4.1 shows the frequency of strings with *oír* 'hear' and *publicar* 'publish' with passive voice and passive with *se*. These are the numbers for year 2019, accessed in 2021.

A second important reason why Spanish prefers a passive with *se* over a passive with *ser* 'be' is the Naked Noun Constraint (NNC). The NNC states that under normal conditions of stress and intonation, a bare common noun cannot be the preverbal subject in Spanish (Suñer 1982: 209). No speaker of Spanish utters sentence (11b) below because it will violate the NNC. This constraint is at work in other languages as well. Thus, the passive with *ser* in (11b) is impossible in Spanish because it would violate the NNC. The passive *se* sentence in (11c) allows the omission of the <u>verber</u> in sentence (11a). Observe that (11a) can be intransitivized as in (11c) because the **verbed** (*carne de res*) is not in preverbal position, and therefore there is no violation of the NNC (*no se viola el NNC*).

(11) a. (*Nosotros*) *Compramos* **carne de res** *esta semana.*
          'We bought beef this week'.
      b. *Carne de res fue comprada esta semana.
          'Beef was bought this week'.
      c. *Se compró* **carne de res** *esta semana.*
          REFL bought beef this week
          'Beef was bought this week'.

This section has shown why Spanish prefers passive *se* sentences to passives with *ser*. It has also shown that a rule of <u>verber</u> intransitivization explains why Spanish and several other languages (perhaps many other languages) use an intransitivizing pronoun to tell your name. The conclusions for this chapter will retake this point because telling your name in a grammar based on the distinction between <u>verber</u> and **verbed** is just an intransitivization with *se*, like the 11 types discussed in Chapters 2 and 3, and other "types" discussed in this chapter. Moreover, the explanation for sentences (9a-h) double as a suggestion on how to introduce intransitivization with *se* on the first pages of textbooks for teaching Spanish at the elementary level.

4.3. Can we, please, never ever again explain in a textbook for Spanish the *accidental or unplanned se*?

Finally, the activity/accomplishment explanation for *drinking coffee* vs. *drinking your coffee* is the same explanation for (12a-b) below, with a nice kicker. Sentence (12b) is a clear example of the infamous "unplanned or accidental *se*", which presumably reflects in the language the indolence of the Spanish-speaking world when applied to something like *se me olvidó la tarea* 'I forgot my homework', *se me rompieron las gafas* 'I broke my glasses', etc. Such an explanation is impossible with a tank leaking heating oil because heating oil tanks are neither part of the Hispanic culture (no need for much heating) nor can anybody claim that tanks have responsibility or lack of it. As Whitley (2002) put it, explanations like this perpetuate the stereotyping that learning a second language is supposed to eradicate.

(12) a. *Salió **aceite** del tanque.*
        came out oil from the tank
        'Some oil leaked out of the tank'.
      b. *<u>Al tanque</u> <u>se</u> <u>le</u> salió **el aceite**.*
        to the tank-DAT REFL DAT-pronoun came out the oil
        'All (of) the oil leaked out of the tank'.

Now the reader can see how sentence (11c) in §2.3 (*<u>a Vargas Llosa</u> <u>se</u> <u>le</u> dio **el Premio Nóbel***), sentence (6) in §3.1 (*al almuerzo <u>se</u> <u>nos</u> servirá(n) **butifarras***), sentences (12a-g) in § 3.1, and (12b) above are the same type of sentence. Readers can also realize that a better explanation (the same explanation) for all of those sentences contributes to a better understanding of (12b), not an easy sentence for a second language learner of Spanish to grasp. What do these sentences have in common? The <u>se</u> is replacing the <u>verber</u>. In fact, they also share that with all of the sentences with an intransitivizing *se* in this book. If this still seems somewhat difficult to digest, it is because intransitivizing with *se* is a powerful phenomenon in Spanish and in many languages. But the understanding of intransitivization after two or three readings of this book (approximately ten to 30 hours, depending on the familiarity with the issues) will be a few times better than the understanding of "reflexivization" that we have had until now.

Learners of Spanish as a second language can get an idea of their comprehension of intransitivizing *se* if they can determine which of the following four sentences does not make much sense. One of them describes an impossible state of affairs. Many readers should also be able to infer the difference in meaning between each pair of sentences:

(13) a. *Alejandra quedó embarazada.*
  b. *Alejandra se quedó embarazada.*
  c. *La abuela quedó viuda.*
  d. *La abuela se quedó viuda.*

Please stop reading if you would like to discover for yourself the difference before looking at the explanation. Sentence (13a) means that Alejandra became pregnant, a common occurrence. Sentence (13b) would mean that Alejandra never terminated her pregnancy (by delivering her child). This is, of course, an impossible outcome. She could have not stayed pregnant for more than nine months (and perhaps a few days). Sentence (13c) will be the sentence commonly uttered in the following days (perhaps even within a couple of months) after Grandpa passed away. Grandma became a widow in the recent past. Sentence (13d) will be the sentence commonly uttered if Grandma never got married again. That is, she remained a widow for the rest of her life. This author would not be surprised to find out that other scholars (or native speakers) can think of other nuances in meaning associated with these two sentences. This is an invitation to explore further similar sentences.

There surely are many contrasts (sentences with *se* or without it) that have been poorly explained and that will be easier to tackle with <u>verber</u> intransitivization. This chapter will end by leaving the reader with an invitation to be the first to explain some of the examples below, and improve upon the explanation proposed above. A few theses could be written to fine-tune and further clarify some of these points in Spanish and in many other languages with robust intransitivization with an intransitivizing pronoun.

A translation for each sentence will be provided below.

(14) a. **Algunos invitados** *no entraron a la casa.*
  b. **Todos los invitados** *(<u>se</u>) entraron cuando empezó a llover.*
  c. **Ningún invitado** *(<u>se</u>) quedó en el patio.*
  d. *No <u>se</u> <u>me</u> sale* **la baba** *por Taylor Swift.*
  e. *<u>Se</u> <u>me</u> vinieron* **las lágrimas** *cuando leí sobre la muerte de Ivan Sag.*

f. **El perdedor** <u>se</u> *queda con Bieber.*

g. **La abuela** *quedó muy débil después de la cirugía.*

h. **La tía Marina** <u>se</u> *quedó con la abuela en el hospital.*

i. **El garaje** *quedó vuelto un desastre después de la inundación.*

j. **Marcos** <u>se</u> *quedó en la casa porque tiene un examen mañana.*

k. **Marcos** *quedó muy contento con su nuevo corte de pelo.*

l. **El chimichurri** *quedó mejor que nunca.*

m. <u>*A Martina le*</u> *quedó mejor que nunca* **el chimichurri**.

n. *El chimichurri siempre* <u>le</u> *queda mejor* <u>*a Anna*</u> *que* <u>*a Martina*</u>.

o. <u>Se</u> <u>nos</u> *olvidó* **el chimichurri** *en la casa de la abuela.*

p. <u>Se</u> <u>nos</u> *quedó* **el chimichurri** *en la casa de la abuela.*

q. **Este chimichurri** <u>nos</u> *quedó para chuparse los dedos.*

Translation for sentences (14a-q):

(15) a. Some guests did not go inside the house.

b. All of the guests went inside when it began to rain.

c. None of the guests stayed in the patio.

d. I do not drool for Taylor Swift.

e. Tears came to my eyes when I read that Ivan Sag had passed.

f. The Loser keeps Bieber.

g. Grandma was left very weak after her surgery.

h. Aunt Marina stayed with Grandma at the hospital.

i. The garage was turned into a disaster after it flooded.

j. Marcos stayed home because he has a test tomorrow.

k. Marcos is very happy with his new haircut.

l. The chimichurri turned out better than ever.

m. The chimichurri that Martina prepared turned out better than ever.

n. The chimichurri that Anna prepares always turns out better than Martina's.

o. We forgot our chimichurri at Grandma's house.

p. We forgot our chimichurri at Grandma's house.

q. This chimichurri turned out so good that you want to lick your fingers.

4.4. Conclusions

This chapter has shown why Spanish prefers passive *se* sentences to passives with *ser*. It has also shown that a rule of <u>verber</u> intransitivization explains why Spanish and several other languages (perhaps many other languages) use an intransitivizing pronoun to tell your name. Moreover, the explanation for sentences

(9a-h) doubles as a suggestion on how to introduce intransitivization with *se* on the first pages of textbooks for teaching Spanish at the elementary level.

Virtually all textbooks for Spanish, particularly beginning ones, explain passive *se* sentences closer to the last chapter than to the first one. It is a structure not explained until page 350 in a popular textbook for elementary Spanish in the United States. *Me llamo (te llamas/se llama)* appears 11 times from pages two to five. *Se dice* 'it is said' (= 'one says') appears three times on page seven in that textbook. If the explanation outlined in sentences (9a-h) in this chapter is adapted to be presented on the first pages of beginning textbooks for Spanish, students using those textbooks will have an explanation for passive *se* at the beginning of chapter 1 and not on page 350.

If the explanation outlined for sentences (9a-h) seems somewhat ambitious at first, it is more because it is new than because it is difficult. The explanation outlined in sentences (7–9) is a suggestion on how to explain the basic function of telling your name in textbooks for Spanish. More importantly, it is an explanation of the most productive intransitivizing rule in the language. Teaching verber intransitivization at the beginning of elementary textbooks is an investment that will pay off for students during the rest of their learning of Spanish as a second language. As Chapter 5 shows, the productivity of the "reflexive" pronoun as an intransitivizing pronoun is a rule common "in a great many languages", to borrow the wording from Perlmutter & Postal (1983: 106) referring to impersonal passives. As for teachers, I will quote from one of my undergraduate students (Mary Kathryn Ball) presenting at a conference in Raleigh, North Carolina, in 2017, "I had studied Spanish since Kindergarten. When I understood verber and **verbed** in college, grammar really made sense for the first time".

As a scholar and a native speaker of Spanish, this author has spent hundreds (perhaps more than 1,000 hours) trying to understand intransitivizing *se* over a period of 30 years. One student in an undergraduate seminar (Lauren Gielinski) told this author in 2021 that it took her about five hours to read this manuscript, plus almost two hours working on the exercises. She then presented this explanation of intransitivizing *se* to the class. The way she presented it to the class is very close to what I would have done. I mention this because an understanding of intransitivization with *se* that took me at least 1,000 hours is now accessible to L2 learners in a fraction of that time. Of course, she does not have my understanding. But any scholar can come very close to my understanding in a fraction of the time that it took me to do so. Thus, in a clear sense, this book is a gift to all speakers of languages with robust reflexive constructions, and especially to those learning one or more of those languages as a second language. As Chapter 5 shows, this author was able to gather intransitivized sentences with a "reflexive" pronoun in 30 languages in the last six to eight weeks of this book's writing. That compilation was a fraction of the work done during those two months. This suggests that the number of languages with <u>verber</u> intransitivization similar to the one in Spanish is easily at least one hundred. Perhaps a few hundreds or even more.

4.5. Exercises

Exercise 1. These sentences come from compositions written by college students of Spanish as a second language. Add the correct form of the intransitivizing pronoun when needed, or omit it, when it cannot be there. Some sentences are correct. A few sentences were added to show a contrast that will help learners understand the need for the intransitivizing pronoun or when it cannot be used. Answers at the end of the exercise.

1   Los datos no se mienten.
2   El crimen está aumentando.
3   El lector se puede ver que el autor no está de acuerdo con esas afirmaciones.
4   Le contestó que consideraría reunir con él, si él se escogía un lugar apropiado.
5   Un catarro cura en una semana con antibióticos y en ocho días sin ellos.
6   Un joven acercó corriendo a la viuda.
7   Los médicos no se curan; uno mismo cura.
8   De los médicos, líbreme Dios, que de las enfermedades libro yo.
9   El proceso se ocurre de nuevo.
10   El tren se salió a las 6:00 de la tarde.
11   En español se usa el artículo definido mucho más que en inglés.
12   El español se usa el artículo definido mucho más que en inglés.
13   La fiebre generalmente cura sin medicina.
14   En inglés, el sujeto precede al verbo y no puede omitir.
15   Es probable que algunos grupos musicales se contribuyan a la violencia.
16   El médico refirió al paciente a otro médico.
17   El médico se refirió al paciente en un estudio longitudinal.
18   El territorio de los Estados Unidos extiende desde Maine hasta Alaska.
19   Con esta decisión prohibió la venta de armas de alta tecnología.
20   Por las anteriores razones, propongo que la siesta debe implementar en los Estados Unidos.
21   El debate sobre la diversidad en la universidad caracteriza por algo interesante.
22   El sistema de raíces de otro tipo de vegetación va a romper.
23   Es un sistema económico en el cual uno beneficia del empobrecimiento de otro.
24   La inestabilidad empeorará.

25 Con este sistema, usted puede conectar en la red y hablar con otros.
26 La fiesta de la nieve de Bariloche celebra con fuegos artificiales.
27 Muchos turistas se esperan la salida de los toros.
28 Muchos turistas se arriesgan la vida.
29 Uno se puede intentar hacerse algo y no llegar a serlo.
30 Uno puede intentar hacer algo y no llegar a hacerlo.
31 Este problema debe considerar con seriedad.
32 Si decimos "ayer había un concierto", no sabe si el concierto ocurrió o no.
33 Ahora nos referimos a un grupo de gente que ha vuelto pesimista gradualmente.
34 Nos esperamos que esta exposición sea de su agrado.
35 El español puede variarse este orden; pero el inglés, no.
36 En español puede variar este orden; pero en inglés, no.
37 Durante esa administración, redujo mucho el crimen en la ciudad.
38 Durante esta administración, disminuyó mucho el crimen en la ciudad.
39 El médico reunió con otros médicos para consultar con ellos.
40 Este ejercicio completó exitosamente.

Exercise 2. The task of the reader is to understand the meaning of each sentence. Warning! A few of these sentences are semantically anomalous. The meaning intended is highly unlikely. Most of these sentences have an intransitivizing pronoun and a <u>verbee</u> (an indirect object). When there is a true <u>verbee</u> in a sentence, there can always be a pronoun duplicating it. Thus, readers who understand the contribution to the meaning of the intransitivizing pronoun and that a <u>verbee</u> means that the participant gained or lost something (the meaning of an indirect object) can understand the meaning of most of these sentences, even if they are new to them. Answers provided after the exercise.

1 <u>Al profesor le</u> salió **sangre** por la nariz.
2 <u>Al profesor se le</u> salió **la sangre** por la nariz.
3 <u>Al profesor se le</u> escapó **un gato**.
4 Al almuerzo <u>se nos</u> servirán **camarones**.
5 No <u>se te</u> olvide **comprar leche** cuando vuelvas para la casa.
6 ¿<u>Se te</u> ocurre **una idea**?
7 ¿<u>Te</u> ocurrió una idea?
8 ¿<u>Te</u> ocurrió **un accidente**?
9 ¿Se te ocurrió un accidente?
10 <u>Al niño le</u> salió **un diente**.
11 <u>Al abuelo se le</u> cayó **un diente**.
12 <u>Al abuelo le</u> cayó **un diente**.
13 <u>Al abuelo le</u> salió **un diente**.
14 <u>Al abuelo se le</u> cayeron **los dientes**.
15 <u>A la abuela se le</u> fue **la mano** en la sal.

4.6. Answers to the exercises

Answers to exercise 1. Strikethrough means that the intransitivizing pronoun must be omitted. An intransitivizing pronoun in capital letters means that it must be added.

1   Los datos no ~~se~~ mienten.
2   El crimen está aumentando.
3   El lector ~~se~~ puede ver que el autor no está de acuerdo con esas afirmaciones.
4   Le contestó que consideraría reunirSE con él, si él ~~se~~ escogía un lugar apropiado.
5   Un catarro SE cura en una semana con antibióticos y en ocho días sin ellos.
6   Un joven SE acercó corriendo a la viuda.
7   Los médicos no ~~se~~ curan; uno mismo SE cura.
8   De los médicos, líbreme Dios, que de las enfermedades ME libro yo.
9   El proceso ~~se~~ ocurre de nuevo.
10 El tren ~~se~~ salió a las 6:00 de la tarde.
11 En español se usa el artículo definido mucho más que en inglés.
12 El español ~~se~~ usa el artículo definido mucho más que el inglés.
13 La fiebre generalmente SE cura sin medicina.
14 En inglés, el sujeto precede al verbo y no puede omitirSE.
15 Es probable que algunos grupos musicales ~~se~~ contribuyan a la violencia.
16 El médico refirió al paciente a otro médico.
17 El médico se refirió al paciente en un estudio longitudinal.
18 El territorio de los Estados Unidos SE extiende desde Maine hasta Alaska.
19 Con esta decisión SE prohibió la venta de armas de alta tecnología.
20 Por las anteriores razones, propongo que la siesta debe implementarSE en los Estados Unidos.
21 El debate sobre la diversidad en la universidad SE caracteriza por algo interesante.
22 El sistema de raíces de otro tipo de vegetación SE va a romper. (Also: va a romperse.)
23 Es un sistema económico en el cual uno SE beneficia del empobrecimiento de otro.
24 La inestabilidad empeorará.
25 Con este sistema, usted puede conectarSE en la red y hablar con otros.
26 La fiesta de la nieve de Bariloche SE celebra con fuegos artificiales.
27 Muchos turistas ~~se~~ esperan la salida de los toros.
28 Muchos turistas ~~se~~ arriesgan la vida.
29 Uno ~~se~~ puede intentar hacerse algo y no llegar a serlo.
30 Uno puede intentar hacer algo y no llegar a hacerlo.
31 Este problema debe considerarSE con seriedad. (Also: SE debe considerar. . .)

32 Si decimos "ayer había un concierto", no SE sabe si el concierto ocurrió o no.
33 Ahora nos referimos a un grupo de gente que SE ha vuelto pesimista gradualmente.
34 ~~Nos~~ Esperamos que esta exposición sea de su agrado.
35 El español puede variar~~se~~ este orden; pero el inglés, no.
36 En español puede variarSE este orden; pero en inglés, no.
37 Durante esa administración, SE redujo mucho el crimen en la ciudad.
38 Durante esta administración, disminuyó mucho el crimen en la ciudad.
39 El médico SE reunió con otros médicos para consultar con ellos.
40 Este ejercicio SE completó exitosamente.

Answers to exercise 2

1 <u>Al profesor le</u> salió **sangre** por la nariz. Some blood came out the professor's nose.
2 <u>Al profesor se le</u> salió **la sangre** por la nariz. The professor lost all of his blood through his nose.
3 <u>Al profesor se le</u> escapó **un gato**. One of the professor's cats escaped.
4 Al almuerzo <u>se nos</u> servirán **camarones**. We will be served shrimp at lunch.
5 No <u>se te</u> olvide **comprar leche** cuando vuelvas para la casa. Don't forget to buy some milk when you are returning home.
6 ¿Se <u>te</u> ocurre **alguna idea**? Does any idea occur to you?
7 ¿Te ocurrió una idea? Semantically anomalous. (Lit: An idea happened to you?)
8 ¿<u>Te</u> ocurrió **un accidente**? An accident happened to you?
9 ¿Se te ocurrió un accidente? Semantically odd (Lit: Did an accident occur to you?)
10 <u>Al niño le</u> salió **un diente**. The child is teething. (One of his teeth is coming out).
11 <u>Al abuelo se le</u> cayó **un diente**. One of Grandpa's teeth fell. (Grandpa lost a tooth.)
12 <u>Al abuelo le</u> cayó **un diente**. Semantically odd (Lit: a tooth dropped on Grandpa).
13 <u>Al abuelo le</u> salió **un diente**. Semantically odd (Lit: Grandpa is teething. One of his teeth is coming out).
14 <u>Al abuelo se le</u> cayeron **los dientes**. Grandpa's dentures fell. Also: Grandpa lost all of his teeth.
15 <u>A la abuela se le</u> fue **la mano** en la sal. Grandma got carried away with the salt. She put too much salt (on what she was cooking).

Notes

1 Throughout this book, the <u>verber</u> is <u>underlined</u>; the verbed is in **bold**; and the <u>verbee</u> (the indirect object) is <u>double-underlined</u>.
Specialized or key terms are written in CAPITAL LETTERS the first time they appear or when their mention is particularly relevant. Capitalized terms will be explained briefly as needed, either in the text itself or in endnotes like this one.
2 The VERBERLESS VERBS of English are: *appeal(1), appear, be, belong, cost, die, fall, happen, matter, occur, remain, seem, sound (1)*. These verbs do not have a <u>verber</u>. **Faller*, **dier*, **belonger*, **matterer* are not nouns in English. See González (2021: Chapter 4 and Chapter 5 for an explanation of verberless sentences in English and in Spanish, respectively). The notation *appeal(1)* means that this is one of two *appeal* verbs in English. One with <u>verber</u> and **verbed** (*<u>the defendant</u> appealed **the decision***) and one with **verbed** and <u>verbee</u> (*does **a trip to the mountains** appeal <u>to you</u>?*). The same for *sound* (*<u>they</u> sounded **an alarm*** and ***a frappuccino** sounds great <u>to me</u>!*).
3 A Google search on 2/20/2017 returned these results:

   (i)   El abuelo cayó = 812
   (ii) El abuelo se cayó = 8,280

   These results are preliminary and not very reliable. Apparently, there is a criminal called "El abuelo". That could have distorted the results. The point of these "numbers" is to invite scholars to do corpus work on some of the sentences discussed in this book.

References

González, Luis H. 2021. *The fundamentally simple logic of language: Learning a second language with the tools of the native speaker*. London: Routledge.

Maldonado, Ricardo. [1999]2006. *A media voz. Problemas conceptuales del clítico* se. México, DF: Universidad Nacional Autónoma de México.

Ngram Viewer. 2019. Google books ngram viewer. http://books.google.com/ngrams. (Last accessed in 2021).

Perlmutter, David M. & Postal, Paul M. 1983. The 1-advancement exclusiveness law. In Perlmutter, David M. & Rosen, Carol G. (eds.), *Studies in relational grammar*, vol. 2, 81–125. Chicago: The University of Chicago Press.

Suñer, Margarita. 1982. *Syntax and semantics of Spanish presentational sentence types*. Washington, DC: Georgetown University Press.

Whitley, M. Stanley. 2002. *Spanish/English contrasts: A course in Spanish linguistics*. 2nd edn. Washington, DC: Georgetown University Press.

Whitley, M. Stanley & González, Luis. 2016. *Gramática para la composición*. 3rd edn. Washington, DC: Georgetown University Press.

5 Bringing together coreference reflexives, decausative reflexives, impersonal passives, and inherently reflexive verbs

5.1. How verber intransitivization brings together coreference reflexives, decausative reflexives, impersonal *se*, and inherently reflexive verbs

COREFERENCE REFLEXIVES are sentences in which the verber and the **verbed** or the verber and the verbee are the same participant, as when *Lauren se baña* '**Lauren** bathes (herself)', *Lauren se viste* '**Lauren** dresses (herself)', Lauren se pone **labial** 'Lauren puts **lipstick** on', *Lauren se cepilla los dientes* 'Lauren brushes **her teeth**', etc.[1] DECAUSATIVE REFLEXIVES are sentences that can omit the verber if replaced with an intransitivizing pronoun, as in *la puerta se abrió* 'the door opened'. IMPERSONAL SE sentences are sentences whose verber is replaced with an intransitivizing pronoun, and that pronoun can be glossed as 'people', 'one', 'you', as in *se trabaja mucho en la universidad* 'people, one, you work(s) a lot in college'. INHERENTLY REFLEXIVE VERBS or mandatorily reflexive verbs are a few verbs in a given language that cannot be used without a reflexive pronoun, as in *Marcos se arrepintió* 'Marcos repented' (cf. **Marcos arrepintió*), *Marcos se atrevió a preparar chimichurri por primera vez* 'Marcos dared to prepare *chimichurri* for the first time', etc. The equivalent in one language of an inherently reflexive verb is not necessarily inherently reflexive in another language. For example, *suicidarse* is the prototypical inherently reflexive verb in Spanish, but it is *commit suicide* in English. Consider sentences (1a-q) below:

(1) a. *Lauren abrió la puerta*.
  'Lauren opened the door'.
  b. **La puerta** fue abierta. (A passive voice sentence)
  'The door was opened'.
  c. *La puerta se abrió*. (A decausative sentence = a passive *se* sentence)
  The door REFL opened[2]
  'The door was opened'; 'the door opened'.

DOI: 10.4324/9781003214090-5

d. *~~Lauren~~ vistió **a Lauren**.
'Lauren dressed Lauren'.

e. ***Lauren** s̲e̲ vistió.*   (A coreference reflexive = a "true" reflexive
sentence)
Lauren REFL dressed
'Lauren dressed (herself)'; 'Lauren got dressed'.

f. **~~Lauren~~ *le puso **desodorante** a Lauren.*
Lauren DAT-pronoun put deodorant to Lauren-DAT
*'Lauren put deodorant on Lauren'.

g. *Lauren s̲e̲ puso **desodorante**.*   (A coreference REFL = a "true"
reflexive sentence)
Lauren REFL put deodorant
'Lauren put deodorant on'.

h. *La Universidad l̲e̲ dio **un premio** a Beatrice.*
la universidad DAT-pronoun gave an award to Beatrice-DAT
'The University gave Beatrice an award'.

i. *A Beatrice s̲e̲ l̲e̲ dio **un premio**.*
to Beatrice-DAT REFL DAT-pronoun gave an award
'Beatrice was given a prize'.

j. *Marcos rompió **una camisa vieja** para limpiar los zapatos.*
'Marcos tore an old shirt to clean his shoes with it'.

k. **Marcos l̲e̲ rompió **la camisa** a Marcos en un clavo.*
Marcos DAT-pronoun tore the shirt to Marcos-DAT on a nail
'Marcos$_i$ tore Marcos$_i$ the shirt on a nail'.

l. *Marcos s̲e̲ rompió **la camisa** en un clavo.*
Marcos REFL tore the shirt on a nail
'Marcos tore his shirt on a nail'.

m. *A Marcos s̲e̲ l̲e̲ rompió **la camisa** en un clavo.*
to Marcos-DAT REFL DAT-pronoun tore the shirt on a nail
'Marcos tore his shirt on a nail'.

n. *En la universidad s̲e̲ trabaja mucho.* (impersonal passive sentence)
in the college REFL work a lot
'In college, people/you/one work(s) a lot'.

o. **En la universidad trabaja mucho.*

p. **Marcos** s̲e̲ arrepintió.
Marcos REFL repented
'Marcos repented'.

q. **Marcos arrepintió.*

It is uncontroversial that the intransitivizing pronoun in sentences like
(1c) above indicates that the ve̲r̲be̲r̲ was omitted. Sentence (1b) is a passive with *ser* 'be', plus the past participle of the main verb (a sentence in

the passive voice). Sentence (1c) is a "passive with *se*" sentence. Remember from Chapter 2 that an analysis in terms of subject, direct object, and indirect object will require three different rules to account for sentences (1c,e,g). On the other hand, an analysis in terms of <u>verber</u> intransitivization requires a single rule for the three sentences. Furthermore, an analysis in terms of subject and direct object and in which one of the arguments (participants) is absorbed (Grimshaw 1990: 154; Marantz 1984: 154–156; among others) has some difficulty in accounting for the intransitivization in sentences like (1g,l) because those sentences have an intransitivizing pronoun, yet they are still "transitive" in the sense that they have a "SURFACE" nominative (the subject) and a "SURFACE" accusative (the direct object).

Going back to sentences (1e,g,l), to the naked eye (e.g. on the surface), *Lauren* or *Marcos* is a "regular" subject in their respective sentence. In fact, the traditional intuition is that when the direct object (DO) or the indirect object (IO) is identical to the subject, that repetition is avoided by replacing the DO or IO with the corresponding reflexive pronoun. In terms currently used in almost all textbooks and by most linguists, sentences (1e,g,l) have a surface subject. In fact, true reflexivization (reflexivization in meaning, as in 1e,g,l) has led scholars since Latin (and perhaps since Greek grammar and before) to believe that the reflexive pronoun is replacing **Lauren** (the DO in 1e), <u>Lauren</u> (the IO in 1g), or <u>Marcos</u> (the IO in 1l). On the other hand, an analysis in terms of <u>verber</u> deletion explains why we still seem to have a "transitive" sentence (in terms of subject and DO in 1l,g). In terms of <u>verber</u> and **verbed**, we have an intransitive sentence because we have a **verbed**, but we do not have a <u>verber</u> (González 2021: 6). As §2.3 explained, a "reflexive" pronoun intransitivizes a sentence by replacing one participant (by forcing the omission of the <u>verber</u>). The <u>Lauren</u> and the <u>Marcos</u> in preverbal position are topicalized indirect objects; that is, they are indirect objects promoted to subject. Clear evidence for that is sentence (1i), an entailment from (1h). Interestingly, what is missing in (1i) is *la universidad* 'college' (the giver). Readers who know Spanish will agree that if someone asks why Beatrice is celebrating, the sentence in (1i) is a felicitous answer.[3]

The answer *A Beatrice le dio un premio* would be a sentence missing a participant (the giver) because such a sentence would require some previous knowledge about the identity of the giver. However, a sentence like *A Beatrice se le dio un premio* presupposes that the listener/reader knows Beatrice, and since the *se* is satisfying or "saturating" (in the sense of Webelhut 1992: 11) the slot of the <u>verber</u>, there is no need to know really who the giver is. In other words, the sentence *A Beatrice se le dio un premio* can be the first sentence in a conversation without any previous context, but the sentence *A Beatrice le dio un premio* cannot.

For theories in which the corresponding intransitivizing pronoun presumably replaces the direct object (or the indirect object) when identical to the subject but replaces the subject in decausative sentences (1c), the fact that the "decausative" pronoun is identical to the reflexive pronoun seems an unexpected coincidence. On the other hand, if an intransitivizing pronoun replaces the <u>verber</u> in a sentence, as argued in González (2021: Chapter 2) and in this book, the fact that said intransitivizing pronoun is the same in coreference reflexives (sentences in which the <u>verber</u> = the **verbed** or the <u>verber</u> = the <u>verbee</u>) and in decausative sentences is expected.

Furthermore, the same intransitivizing pronoun is also used in impersonal passive sentences (1n). As Perlmutter & Postal (1983: 107) observed, impersonal passives can be derived only from unergative verbs; that is, from intransitive verbs whose only participant is agentive. In other words, impersonal passive sentences are possible with verbs whose only participant is the <u>verber</u>. The fact that the impersonal passive pronoun is the intransitivizing pronoun in many languages is also expected if the <u>verber</u> in a sentence can be omitted provided it is replaced with the corresponding intransitivizing pronoun. Sentence (1n) above is an intransitive sentence whose only participant is the <u>verber</u>. As explained in §2.3, even an intransitive sentence can be intransitivized by one participant if its only participant is a <u>verber</u>.

Finally, there are a few inherently reflexive verbs in many languages. If *Marcos repented*, he is the <u>repenter</u> and the **repented**. You can forgive someone else, but you cannot repent them. If *Marcos se ausentó* 'Marcos absented' (cf. *Marcos ausentó), he is the <u>absenter</u> and the **absentee** (the absented person). See González (2021: 38–39) for an explanation of why the nominalization of a **verbed** is done in English with the morphology of a <u>verbee</u>. That is *leísmo* in English. An interviewed candidate is an interviewee; a nominated person is a nominee. However, a <u>grantee</u> is different from the **granted money**; a <u>licensee</u> is different from the **licensed product/ service**, etc.

Interestingly, inherently reflexives (verbs that have to be always used with a reflexive pronoun) have the same intransitivizing pronoun used in sentences (1c,e,g,l,n). That is somewhat expected because in a sense, those verbs have a participant "doubly" involved in the event, a state of affairs not easy to see in all inherently reflexive verbs. A person who commits suicide is the killer and the killed. It is easier to see the two participants in inherently reflexive verbs if we consider a few verbs of movement with animate and inanimate participants.

Before we discuss the following example, the reader is invited to ponder two questions. First, is the mail the <u>arriver</u> or the **arrived**? Readers familiar with the UNACCUSATIVE HYPOTHESIS will not have to think much to answer this question.[4]

Second, is the mail person the <u>arriver</u> or the **arrived**? Readers who might not be sure now will be able to answer these two questions after the following discussion. Consider who/what is the <u>mover</u> and who/what is the **moved** in (2a,b). The <u>verber</u> and the **verbed** are not coded to give readers a chance to see the difference for themselves.

(2) a. Kate moved the table to a corner of the room.
     b. Kate moved to a corner of the room.

The answer is different for (2a) and (2b). It is uncontroversial that <u>Kate</u> is the mover and **the table** is the moved in (2a). What about (2b)? With the <u>verber</u> and the **verbed** entailments *and with world knowledge*, we can see why Kate is the mover and the moved. She passes both the <u>verber</u> entailment and the **verbed** entailment. If it is true that Kate moved to a corner of the room, it is also true that she is the mover; that is, she is the one doing some moving. She is changing her location to a corner of the room. In addition, if (2b) is true, it is also true that she is the moved. Thus, the table is the moved in (2a), but in (2b), Kate is <u>the mover</u> and **the moved**.

Now it will be easier to understand why in Italian the auxiliary in (3a) is *avere* 'have', but the one for (3b) is *essere* 'be'. Sentences (2a,b) help readers understand why Luisa is the runner in (3a), but she is the runner and the run in (3b). The sentences in (3a,b) from Italian are discussed in Van Valin & LaPolla (1997: 416). They come originally from Centineo (1986):

(3) a. *Luisa ha cor-so*   (Activity)
         have-3sgPRES run-PSTP
         'Luisa has run'.
     b. *Luisa è cor-s-a a casa*
         be 3sgPRES run-PSPT-Fsg to house
         'Luisa has run home'.

It is uncontroversial that sentence (3a) expresses an activity and if Luisa ran, she was the runner. In fact, one can add to sentence (3a) *nel parco* 'in the park'. One can also add *per 30 minuti* 'for 30 minutes', an adverbial used as a test to distinguish an activity from an accomplishment (*Luisa ha corso nel parco per 30 minuti* 'Luisa has ran in the park for 30 minutes'). On the other hand, if *Luisa è corsa a casa in 30 minuti* 'Luisa has run home in 30 minutes', she is the runner and she is the run. By the way, readers familiar with Aktionsart classes (Dowty 1991; Van Valin & LaPolla 1997; Vendler 1957; among many others) will recognize that *per 30 minuti* 'for 30 minutes' and *in 30 minuti* 'in 30 minutes' are tests for activities and for accomplishments, respectively. There are several interesting connections to be discussed with this example. But the main point here is to show that an animate subject with a verb of movement is the <u>verber</u> and the **verbed**.

After this discussion, readers from languages with inherently reflexive verbs without an intransitivizing pronoun will have a better understanding of verbs like *arrepentirse* 'repent', *atreverse*, 'dare', *ausentarse* 'to absent oneself, to be absent', *quejarse* 'complain', *suicidarse* 'commit suicide', etc. Whitley (2002: 176) observes that English has three inherently reflexive verbs: avail oneself, perjure oneself, pride oneself. *Absent oneself* is also an inherently reflexive verb. It is conceivable that there are a few other such verbs in English. Interestingly, *suicidarse* is 'commit suicide', but *cometer perjurio* is 'perjure oneself'. A mirror effect in the two languages, as the late Jorge Luis Borges would probably have observed.

This section has shown that a "separation" of coreference reflexive sentences ("truly reflexive" sentences), as in (1e,g,l) and other "types" of reflexives is an intuitive distinction, but a distinction on the wrong track. That distinction, based on a grammar based on subject and direct object, cannot explain why the pronoun used for countless non reflexive sentences in Spanish (and in other languages, as §5.2 will show), is the same pronoun used in coreference reflexive sentences. On the other hand, a rule of <u>verber</u> intransitivization shows why the pronoun is the same and why coreference reflexive sentences are a special case of <u>verber</u> intransitivization and not the other way around, as Chapter 3 showed.

The following section shows sentences similar to some of the 11 sentences in Spanish from Chapter 3 in these ten languages: Catalan, French, German, Italian, Korean, Latin, Polish, Portuguese, Romanian, and Russian. The sentences in Spanish are repeated here for convenience. Korean is included as a point of reference. Thanks to all of the informants who provided sentences in these ten languages. After these ten sets of sentences, there will be smaller sets of sentences (one to four sentences) in 20 other languages.

5.2. The 11 types of intransitivized sentences with a reflexive pronoun in Spanish (§ 3.1) and in ten other languages

I could not find a taxonomy in other languages similar to the 11 types of sentences in Spanish. Therefore, I asked several native speakers (or near-native speakers, in two cases) of a few languages to provide the equivalent of the 11 types in their native language. This section has those sentences. §5.3 will have one to four different sentences with an intransitivizing pronoun in 20 different languages. Examples from languages featured in this section will be included if they are relevant. For example, a native speaker of Spanish will find remarkable similarities between the "reflexive" sentences in Kannada and Spanish in Lidz (1996: 27–28).

Remember that the <u>verber</u> is underlined, the **verbed** is in bold, and the <u>verbee</u> is double-underlined.

(4) **Spanish.** From §3.1. A translation for each sentence is offered after the examples.

a. **Olga** <u>se</u> vio en el espejo.	True reflexive *se* (of a direct object)
b. <u>Olga</u> <u>se</u> compró **una blusa**.	True reflexive (of an indirect object)
c. <u>Se</u> caminó todo el día.	Impersonal *se*
d. <u>Se</u> cierra **la puerta** a la 1:00 PM.	Passive *se* (= **este edificio** <u>se</u> remodeló)
e. <u>Rosa</u> <u>se</u> cortó **el pelo**; <u>Juan</u> <u>se</u> operó ayer.	Causative *se*
f. Al almuerzo <u>se</u> <u>nos</u> servirá(n) **butifarras**.	"Unplanned or accidental *se*"
g. **El aluminio** <u>se</u> ha fundido.	Intransitivizing *se*
h. **Ellos** <u>se</u> aburrieron (de la tele).	Reflexive *se* of emotional reaction
i. **Ustedes** <u>se</u> casaron.	"Reciprocal" *se*
j. **Ella** <u>se</u> quejó de la sopa.	Inherent or lexical or *se*
k. <u>Ella</u> <u>se</u> bebió **el café**.	Meaning-changing/inchoative *se*

The translation for each sentence is as follows: (a) Olga saw herself in the mirror. (b) Olga bought a blouse (for herself). (c) People/one walked all day. (d) Someone closes the door at 1:00 PM; the door gets closed at 1:00 PM. (e) Rosa cut her hair; Juan had surgery yesterday (he was operated on). (f) We will be served Catalan sausage at lunch. (g) The aluminum has melted. (h) They got bored (from watching TV). (i) You (two) got married. (j) She complained about the soup. (k) She drank her coffee.

(5) **Catalan.** Sentences provided by Laia Vancells López, PC, 2021.
   a. L'Olga es va mirar al mirall.
   b. L'Olga es va comprar una brusa.
   c. Es va caminar tot el dia.
   d. Es tanca la porta a la 1:00 PM.
   e. La Rosa es va tallar el cabell; El Juan es va operar ahir.
   f. A l'esmorzar se'ns servirà botifarres.
   g. L'alumini s'ha fos.
   h. Ells es van avorrir.

i. Vostès es van casar.
j. Ella es va queixar de la sopa.
k. Ella es va beure el cafè.

Sentences with an intransitivizing pronoun: (5a-k). Eleven sentences.

(6) **French.** Examples provided by Dr. Judy Kem, PC, 2021.
   a. Olga s'est vue dans le miroir.
   b. Olga s'est acheté un chemisier.
   c. On se promène toute la journée.
   d. La porte se ferme à une heure de l'après-midi.
   e. Rosa s'est coupée les cheveux; Juan s'est fait opéré.
   f. N/A?
   g. L'aluminium s'est fondu.
   h. Ils se sont ennuyés de la télé. [This is an odd sentence. One would say "La télé m'ennuie" instead.]
   i. Vous vous êtes marié(e).
   j. Elle s'est plainte de la soupe.
   k. Elle a bu le café. N/A.

Sentences with an intransitivizing pronoun: (6a,b,d,e,g,i,j). Seven sentences. Perhaps (6h) as well.

(7) **German.** Examples provided by Sofia Rothberger-Kraal, PC, 2021.
   a. Olga sieht sich im Spiegel.
   b. Olga kaufte sich eine Bluse
   c. Man wandert hier den ganzen Tag. Hier wird um ein Uhr geschlossen.
   d. Wir schliessen or (with the proper letter ß = sz symbol) wir schließen um ein Uhr.
   e. Rosa ließ sich ihre Haare schneiden lassen. Rosa hat sich ihre Haare schneiden lassen. Gestern hatte Juan sich operieren lassen.
   f. Uns werden Würstchen serviert zum Mittagessen. Zum Mittagessen werden uns Würstchen serviert.
   g. Das Aluminium hat sich geschmolzen.
   h. Sie haben sich gelangweilt. Der Fernseher hat sich gelangweilt. (Der Fernseher is the person who watches TV).
   i. Sie sind verheiratet (= they are married).
   j. Sie hat sich über die Suppe beklagt.
   k. Sie hat den Kaffee getrunken.

Sentences with an intransitivizing pronoun: (7a,b,e,g,h,i,j). Seven sentences.

(8) **Italian.** Examples provided by Silvia Tiboni-Craft, PC, 2021.
   a. Olga si è vista allo specchio.
   b. Olga si è comprata una camicetta.
   c. Si è camminato tutto il giorno.
   d. La porta si chiude alle 13:00.
   e. Rosa si è tagliata i capelli; Juan è stato operato ieri.
   f. A pranzo si serviranno le salsicce **or** A pranzo verranno servite le salsicce.
   g. L'alluminio si è sciolto.
   h. Si sono annoiati (della TV).
   i. Vi siete sposati.
   j. Si è lamentata della zuppa.
   k. Si è bevuta il caffé.

Sentences with an intransitivizing pronoun: (8a-k). Eleven sentences.

(9) **Korean.** Examples provided by Dr. Hosun Kim, PC, 2021.
   a. **Olga** se vio en el espejo.
      K: 올가는 거울을 보았다./올가는 거울속의 자신을 보았다.
      Olga saw mirror./Olga saw herself in mirror.
   b. Olga se compró **una blusa**.
      K: 올가는 브라우스를 샀다.
      Olga bought blouse.
   c. Se caminó todo el día.
      K: 사람들은 하루종일 걸었다.
      The people walked all day.
   d. Se cierra **la puerta** a la 1:00 PM.
      K: 오후 한시에 문을 닫는다.
      Close door at 1:00 PM.
   e. Rosa se cortó **el pelo.**
      K: 로사는 머리를 잘랐다.
      Rosa cut hair.
   f. Al almuerzo se nos servirá(n) **butifarras.**
      K: 점심에 소시지가 나왔다.
      At lunch came out/served butifarra.
   g. **El aluminio** se ha fundido.
      K: 알루미늄이 녹았다.
      melted aluminium

h. **Ellos** <u>se</u> aburrieron (de la tele).
   K: 그들은 지루해졌다.
   They became to be bored.
i. **Ustedes** <u>se</u> casaron.
   K: 당신들은 결혼하였다.
   You married.
j. **Ella** <u>se</u> quejó de la sopa.
   K: 그녀는 슆에 대해 불평했다.
   She made complaint about soup.
k. <u>Ella</u> <u>se</u> bebió **el café**.
   K: 그녀는 커피를 전부 마셔버렸다.
   She drank all coffee.

According to Dr. Hosun Kim, Korean does not intransitivize with a reflexive pronoun.

(10) **Latin.** Sentences provided by Jessie Craft, PC, 2021.
   a. Olga se in speculo vidit.
   b. Olga (sibi) stolam emit.
   c. Totum diem ambulavit.
   d. Hora diei nona ianua clauditur.
   e. Rosa comas reccidit. /Juan sectus est heri.
   f. In prandio nobis farcimina apponentur./Aliquis nobis farcimina apponet.
   g. Aluminium liquefactum est.
   h. Taeduit eos _____. (whatever bored them is expressed either with the verb in its infinitive or the genitive of the noun)
   i. Iuncti estis nuptiis.
   j. Questa est ius.
   k. Bibit caffeam.

Sentences with an intransitivizing pronoun: (10a). Only 1. As pointed out in García (1975: 6–7), Latin had sentences reflexive in meaning ("regular" reflexives, as García calls them), but "the non-reflexive are Spanish (and Romance) innovations".

(11) **Polish.** Sentences provided by Bożenna Furmanek and Dr. Olgierda Furmanek, PC, 2021. (Mother and daughter).
   a. Olga zobaczyła się w lustrze *or* Olga zobaczyła siebie w lustrze.
   b. Olga kupiła sobie bluzkę.
   c. Chodziła sobie cały dzień

    d. Drzwi zamyka się o godz.13.00.
    e. Róża ścięła sobie włosy.
    f. Na śniadanie podadzą nam katalońską kiełbasę.
    g. Aluminium się roztopiło.
    h. Znudzili się (oglądaniem telewizji). *They got bored by watching.*
    i. Pobraliście się.
    j. Poskarżyła się na brata. – She complained about her brother.
       According to the informants, you complain about animates, not
       inanimates. (??Poskarżyła się na zupę).
    k. Wypiła sobie kawę. (Shorter form not possible here).

Remember that the notation "??" is used in Maldonado ([1999]2006: 43)
for *casos marginales* 'marginal cases'.
   Sentences with an intransitivizing pronoun: (11a,b,c,d,e,g,h,i,j,k). Ten
sentences.

(12) **Portuguese.** Sentences provided by Rafael Lima, PC, 2021.
    a. Olga se viu no espelho.
    b. Olga comprou uma blusa.
    c. Caminhou/Caminham o dia todo.
    d. Fechou/Fecham a porta às 13h/ à uma da tarde.
    e. Rosa cortou o cabelo/Rosa cortou o seu próprio cabelo. Juan foi
      operado ontem.
    f. Para o almoço, nos servirá(rão) *butifarras*.
    g. O alumínio se fundiu/derreteu.
    h. Eles se cansaram (de assistir TV).
    i. Vocês se casaram.
    j. Ela se queixou da sopa.
    k. Ela bebeu o (seu) café.

Sentences with an intransitivizing pronoun: (12a,b,g,h,i,j). Six sentences.

(13) **Romanian**. Sentences provided by Dr. Gabriela Cerghedean, PC,
    2021.
    a. Olga s-a văzut in oglindă.
    b. Olga şi-a cumpărat o bluza.
    c. S-a mers toată ziua.
    d. Uşa se închide la 1:00.
    e. Rosa si-a tăiat parul; Juan s-a operat ieri.
    f. Ne vor servi cârnaţi la prânz.
    g. Aluminiu s-a topit.

    h. Ei s-au plictisit.
    i. Voi va-ţi căsătorit.
    j. Ea s-a plîns despre supă.
    k. Ea şi-a băut cafeaua.

Sentences with an intransitivizing pronoun: (13a,b,c,d,e,g,h,i,j,k). Ten sentences.

(14) **Russian.** Sentences provided by Natalia Azarova, PC, 2021.
    a. Ольга увидела себя в зеркале
        Olga saw herself in mirror
    b. Ольга купила себе блузку
        Olga bought herself blouse
    c. Весь день ходили/ходил/ходила и т.п.; [кто-то] Весь день на ногах
        All day (we/I/you) walked; (someone/we/I/you) all day on legs
    d. Дверь запирается/запирают в 13:00ч
        Door gets closed/("they") close at 1PM
    e. Роза постриглась; Хуану сделали операцию вчера
        Rosa cut hair to herself; (to) Juan ("they") made surgery yesterday
    f. На обед (нам) будут подавать колбасу.
        For lunch, (to us) (they) will serve butifarra
    g. Алюминий расплавился
        Aluminum melted itself
    h. N/A
    i. Вы поженились
        You married (wifed!) yourselves
    j. Она пожаловалась на суп
        She complained herself on soup
    k. Она выпила кофе
        She drank coffee
        Sentences with an intransitivizing pronoun: (14a,b,d,e,g,i,j). Seven sentences.

5.3. A smaller set of sentences intransitivized with an intransitivizing pronoun in 20 other languages

The purpose of this final section is to invite scholars or students from any language to explore in more detail intransitivizing with a reflexive pronoun in their language(s). Even if there is a good body of research of intransitivized (reflexivized) sentences in any given language, that research can hopefully be improved with the proposal in this book.

Readers are finally invited to observe that an intransitivizing pronoun that replaces a <u>verber</u> that is omitted not only offers a unified account of "reflexive" sentences. That intransitivizing pronoun is also sometimes very similar even across languages belonging to different families, as sentences from the 30 languages used in this chapter show.

Note on ABBREVIATIONS and GLOSSES in the following examples:

Since the following examples come from five different sources, and sometimes those sources are quoting examples from other scholars, it seemed appropriate to leave those examples exactly as quoted in the last source. Abbreviations used in those sources are not provided. Readers interested in further studying some of the examples will find the abbreviations in the source quoted.

This is a good opportunity to invite scholars to adopt the *Generic style rules for linguistics* (2014), compiled by Martin Haspelmath. This book follows those guidelines, except for small caps, for which this book uses capital letters. www.academia.edu/7370927/The_Generic_Style_Rules_for_Linguistics

Abkhaz (Hewitt 1979: 77; 105; quoted in Haspelmath 2019: 8)
(15) a. *bə-z-bo-yt'*
         2SG.OBJ-1SG.SBJ-see-FIN
         'I see you'.
      b. *lcə̀-l-š-we-yt'*
         REFL.F-3SG.F.SBJ-kill-DYN-FIN
         'She kills herself'.

Bulgarian (Rivero 2003: 471; quoted in Fernández-Soriano & Mendikoetxea 2013: 8)
(16) Na Ivan mu se sčupixa očilata
      John-DAT he-DAT REFL broke 3PL glasses.the
      'John accidentally broke the glasses'.
      (In Spanish: <u>A Juan</u> <u>se</u> <u>le</u> quebraron **los vasos**). ('Glasses' is in Spanish *vasos* or *gafas*)

Chinese (Tang 1989: 98; quoted in Haspelmath 2019: 12)
(17) Mandarin Chinese
      *Zhangsan ai **ta-ziji**.*
      Zhangsan love him-self
      'Zhangsan loves himself'.

Croatian (Van Valin & LaPolla 1997: 409)

(18) a. *Petar-Ø je otvori-o prozor-Ø.*
    – MsNOM be.3sg open-past.Msg window-MsgACC
    'Peter opened the window'.

   b. *Prozor-Ø se otvori-o.*
    Window-MsgNOM REFL.3sg open-PAST.Msg
    'The window opened'.

Diyari (Austin 1981; quoted in Lidz 1996: 18)

(19) a. *ngani muduwa-tadi-yi*
    1SGS scratch-REFL-PRES
    'I scratch myself'.

   b. *nawu mana ngandawalka-tadi-na wara-yi*
    3SGNFS door-ABS close-REFL-PART AUX-PRES
    'The door got closed'.

Finnish (Sells et al. 1987; Geniušiene 1987; both quoted in Lidz 1996: 18)

(20) a. *jussi puolusta-utu-i*
    john defend-REFL-PST
    'John defended himself'

   b. *ovi ava-utu*
    door-NOM open-REFL
    'The door opens'.

Fula (Maldonado [1999]2006: 38)

(21) a. femmb-a
    Shave ACTIVE
    Shave 'afeitar'

   b. Femmb-o
    Shave-MIDDLE
    Get oneself shaved 'darse una afeitada (con el peluquero)'

   c. Femmb-it-o
    Shave-REF-MIDDLE
    Shave oneself 'afeitarse (uno mismo)'

Greek (Linda 1990, 1993; quoted in Maldonado [1999]2006: 119)

(22) a. *i iyia tu me stenaxori* MARCADO (Presented as in Maldonado.
    Gloss in English added)
    NOM salud GEN ACC 3s=preocupar=ACT

"Me preocupa su salud"
'Her health worries me' (Lit: to me, worry her health)
b. *Stenaxoryéme ya tin iyía tu*
1s=preocupar=MD PREP ACC salud GEN
"Me preocupo por su salud"
'I am worried because of her health'.
(This example shows a middle SE (*me*, since it is 1st person in Greek).

Hausa (Newman 2000: 524; quoted in Haspelmath 2019: 20).
(23) a. *Tala taa gan ta a maduubin.*
Tala 3SG.PST see her in mirror
'Tala saw her/herself in the mirror'.
b. *Tala taa ga kanta a maduubin.*
Tala 3SG.PST see herself in mirror
'Tala saw herself in the mirror'.

Imbabura Quechua (Cole 1982; quoted in Lidz 1996: 18)
(24) a. ispiju-pi riku-ri-rka-ni
mirror-in see-REFL-PST-1
'I saw myself in the mirror'.
b. pungu-kuna-ka paska-ri-rka
door-PL-TOP open-REFL-PST.3
'The doors opened'.

Kannada (Amritavalli 1984; quoted in Lidz 1996: 18–19)
(25) a. avan-u tann-annu hoDe-du-koND-a
he-NOM self-ACC hit-PP-REFL.PST-3SM
'He hit himself'.
b. baagil-u muc̆c̆-i-koND-itu
door-NOM close-PP-REFL.PST-3SN
'The door closed'.

Lithuanian. (Geniušiene 1987; quoted in Lidz 1996: 19)
(26) a. *on-a graz̆'ina-si*
ann-NOM adorns-REFL
'Ann adorns herself'.
b. *dur-ys at-si-dare*
door-NOM.PL PERF-REFL-close
'The doors closed'.

Panyjima (Pama-Nyungan; suffix *-pula*). (Dench 1991: 160; quoted in Haspelmath 2019: 8)

(27) *Ngatha wirnta-rna-**pula** jina.*
     1SG.NOM cut-PST-REFL foot
     'I cut myself in the foot'.

Observe that coming from a language like Spanish, this sentence is almost a word-by-word equivalent of (*yo*) *corteme pie*; that is, (*yo*) *me corté un pie* 'I cut myself a foot' ('I cut my foot').

Polish (Haspelmath 2019: 2)

(28) a. *Widziała siebie w lustrze.*
          she.saw self.ACC in mirror
          'She saw herself in the mirror'.
     b. *Jankowi złamały się okulary.*
          JohnDAT brokenFEM-PL Refl glasses (Fernández-Soriano & Mendikoetxea 2013: 8)
          'John accidentally broke the glasses'.
          (A Juan se le rompieron las gafas.) ['Glasses' can be *vasos* or *gafas* in Spanish]
     c. *Woda gotuje **się** bardzo szybko.* (Janic 2020; Quoted in Haspelmath 2019: 22)
          water boil.~~3SG~~ REFL very quickly
          'The water boils very quickly'.

Russian (Babby 1975; quoted in Lidz 1996: 19)

(29) a. *on zastrelil-sja*
          he-NOM shot-REFL
          'He shot himself'
     b. *dver' zakryla-s'*
          door-NOM closed-REFL
          'The door closed'.
     c. On utixomiril sebja. (Haiman 1983; quoted in Maldonado [1999] 2006: 99)
          3s calmar +PST RFL
          Se tranquilizó a sí mismo (volitivo)
          'He calmed himself'. (This author's translation into English)
     d. On utixomiril-sja
          3s calmar+PST-MD
          'Se calmó (en forma natural)'
          'He calmed down' (This author's translation into English).

Swahili (Haspelmath 2019: 8)
(30) a. *a-li-**m**-kata*
   3SG-PST-3SG.OBJ-cut
   'she cut him'
   b. *a-li-**ji**-kata*
   3SG-PST-REFL-cut
   'she cut herself'

Thulung (Trans-Himalayan; suffix *-si*). (Lahaussois 2016: 54; quoted in Haspelmath 2019: 7)
(31) *Memma thʌ-**si**-m sintha koŋŋa je.*
   then hide-REFL-SUFF night only come.out
   'Then he hides (himself) and only comes out at night'.

Turkish (suffix *-n*) [Haspelmath 2019: 7)
(32) *kurula-**n**-dı-m*
   dry-REFL-PST-1SG
   'I dried myself'.

Tzotzil (Mayan language from Chiapas, Mexico. Maldonado ([1999] 2006: 34):
(33) a. *poxta – [o] a- ba*
      Cuidar IMP A2 RFL
      'Cuídate'.
      'Take care of yourself'.
   b. *?i-s- k'al s-ba?ochel*
      PERF A3 apretar A3-RFL adentro
      'Él se metió en un lugar apretado [se apretujó]'.
      'He went inside a tight place'.
   c. *?i- s- ni? s – ba yalel*
      PERF A3 jalar A3-RFL abajo
      'Se estiró [una prenda de vestir]'.
      'Got stretched (a garment)'.
   d. *?i-s-kap s-ba li?ixim – e*
      PERF A3 revolver A3 RFL el maíz cl
      'El maíz se revolvió'.
      'The corn was stirred'. (Translations into English by this author 33a-d)

Ute (Uto-Aztecan). (Givon 2011: 237; quoted in Haspelmath 2019: 12)

(34) *Nanos punikya-qhay-'u.*
self see-ANT-3SG
'She saw herself'.

Yakut (Geniušiene 1987; quoted in Lidz 1996: 19)

(35) a. *kini sime-n-er*
she-ABS dress.up-REFL-3SG.PRES
'She dressed herself up'.

b. *mas tohu-n-na*
stick-ABS break-REFL-3SG.PST
'The stick broke'.

Yavapai (Kendall 1976; quoted in Lidz 1996: 20)

(36) a. *hmañ-c kwe-wiv-v-i*
child-SUBJ thing-clothe-REFL-TNS
'The child dressed himself'

b. *?wa:ta?ami-c skwiñ-v-km*
door-SUBJ lock-REFL-INC
'The door locked'.

5.4. Conclusions

Reflexive constructions have been a formidable challenge for learners of Spanish, including native speakers and scholars. The difficulty comes from a grammar based on grammatical relations (subject, direct object, indirect object), which has made it extremely difficult to see that the GRAMMATI-CAL subject of a coreference reflexive sentence (a "true" reflexive or a "regular" reflexive) is actually the underlying (LOGICAL) **verbed** or ver-bee. The explanation of reflexive constructions based on grammatical relations has resulted in the need to posit multiple functions of *se*, so difficult to tell apart that even scholars cannot agree on them. A grammar based on ver-ber, **verbed**, and verbee accounts with a single rule for all of the sentences with an intransitivizing pronoun discussed in this book: an intransitiviz-ing pronoun shows that the verber of the sentence was replaced. Therefore, this analysis shows that the subject of a coreference reflexive sentence is the **verbed**, which has been unaccusativized (promoted from the accusa-tive or direct object position to the subject position); or the verbee, which has been undativized (promoted from dative or indirect object position to subject position). An intransitivizing pronoun that replaces the <u>verber</u> also explains decausative sentences (*la puerta se abrió* 'the door opened', *el vaso se quebró* 'the glass broke'). This analysis also shows that the subject of a causative sentence with a reflexive pronoun as in <u>Rosa</u> <u>se</u> *cortó* **el pelo** 'Rosa had **her hair** cut' because <u>a hair stylist</u> cut her **hair** (i.e., cut her hair for her) is the underlying <u>verbee</u>, uncontroversial evidence that an intransitivizing pronoun replaces the underlying <u>verber</u> (the hair stylist). Further exploration of this type of causative sentences across languages is one of the most provocative issues for further research stemming out of this proposal.

This chapter also showed that it is easy to find equivalents of some of the 11 types of sentences in Spanish discussed in Chapter 3 in "a great many languages", as Perlmutter & Postal (1983: 106) observed about languages with impersonal passives. The "great" refers, of course, to number. It is a puzzle (Lidz 1996: 146 calls it the "homophony puzzle") that a decausative reflexive pronoun (or marker or morpheme or trace) that replaces the SUBJECT or AGENT in decausative sentences (*la puerta* <u>se</u> *abrió* 'the door opened') is the same as the reflexive pronoun (or marker or morpheme or trace) that presumably replaces the DIRECT OBJECT or the INDIRECT OBJECT in truly reflexive sentences. On the other hand, if that INTRANSITIVIZING pronoun (or marker or morpheme or trace) replaces the <u>VERBER</u> in sentences reflexive in meaning and in many other sentences, then the observation that the marker is the same is not a puzzle at all: the same marker indicates that the same rule has applied. A rule of VERBER INTRANSITIVIZATION that replaces the <u>verber</u> with a pronoun explains why the overwhelming majority of sentences with a "reflexive" pronoun are not reflexive in meaning, why "reflexive" sentences are a special case of <u>verber</u> intransitivization and not the other way around, why passive sentences with *ser* 'be' are synonymous with passive sentences with *se* (when both are possible), and why native speakers do not know or cannot tell apart the half a dozen to a dozen types of sentences with a "reflexive" pronoun that many languages putatively have. Native speakers apply intuitively and implicitly a rule of <u>verber</u> intransitivization the same way they can distinguish subject and direct object (and indirect object) before they go to Kindergarten: because they understand and produce their language by computing a <u>verber</u> entailment and a **verbed** entailment, as proposed in González (2021). If native speakers are computing a <u>verber</u> entailment in their regular use of language, and rules in their language track that <u>verber</u> across variations of sentences (intransitivization rules), native speakers should understand and produce sentences with an intransitivizing pronoun effortlessly, efficiently, and without the need for any instruction. They do.

Notes

1 Throughout this book, the <u>verber</u> is <u>underlined</u>; the verbed is in **bold**; and the <u>verbee</u> (the indirect object) is <u>double-underlined</u>.
    Specialized or key terms are written in CAPITAL LETTERS the first time they appear or when their mention is particularly relevant. Capitalized terms will be explained briefly as needed, either in the text itself or in endnotes like this one.
2 Abbreviations: ACC (accusative); DAT (dative); REFL (reflexive)
3 FELICITOUS: According to Mark Lieberman, "a sentence must not only be grammatical to be correctly performed, it must also be felicitous", or well suited for the purpose. (www.thoughtco.com/felicity-conditions-speech-1690855) [Entry written by Richard Nordquist, 2019]
4 In terms of <u>verber</u> and **verbed**, the UNACCUSATIVY HYPOTHESIS is the discovery that the subject of many sentences is a **verbed**, not a <u>verber</u>. Simplifying somewhat, the unaccusativy hypothesis was proposed by David Perlmutter in terms of subject and direct object in work that began to be published in the late 1970s. Perlmutter himself writes that, "The Unaccusative Hypothesis developed itself in joint work with Paul Postal" (Perlmutter 1978: 185).

References

Centineo, Giulia. 1986. A lexical theory of auxiliary selection in Italian. In *Davis working papers in linguistics*, vol. 1, 1–35. Davis, CA: University of California, Davis.

Dowty, David. 1991. Thematic proto-roles and argument selection. *Language* 67.547–619. www.jstor.org/stable/pdf/415037.

Fernández-Soriano, Olga & Mendikoetxea, Amaya. 2013. Non selected dative arguments in Spanish anticausative constructions. In Seržant, Ilja A. & Kulikov, Leonid (eds.), *The diachronic typology of non-canonical subjects*, 3–34. Amsterdam: John Benjamins Publishing Company. https://doi.org/10.1075/slcs.140.01fer.

García, Erica C. 1975. *The role of theory in linguistic analysis: The Spanish pronoun system*. Amsterdam: North-Holland Publishing Company.

González, Luis H. 2021. *The fundamentally simple logic of language: Learning a second language with the tools of the native speaker*. London: Routledge.

Grimshaw, Jane. 1990. *Argument structure*. Cambridge, MA: The MIT Press.

Haspelmath, Martin. 2019. Comparing reflexive constructions in the world's languages. (Draft version of June 18, 2019). www.academia.edu/39975707/Comparing_reflexive_constructions_in_the_worlds_languages.

Kazenin, Konstantin I. 2001. Verbal reflexives and the middle voice. In *Language typology and language universals: An international handbook*, vol. 2, 916–927. Berlin: De Gruyter. doi:10.1515/9783110171549.2.10.916 (January 21, 2019). (This author did not have access to this work. Reference provided in Haspelmath 2019).

Lidz, Jeffrey L. 1996. *Dimensions of reflexivity*. Newark, DE: University of Delaware. (Doctoral dissertation).

Maldonado, Ricardo. [1999]2006. *A media voz. Problemas conceptuales del clítico se*. México, DF: Universidad Nacional Autónoma de México.

Marantz, Alec. 1984. *On the nature of grammatical relations*. Cambridge, MA: The MIT Press.

Perlmutter, David M. 1978. Impersonal passives and the unaccusative hypothesis. *BLS* 4.157–189.

Perlmutter, David M. & Postal, Paul M. 1983. The 1-advancement exclusiveness law. In Perlmutter, David M. & Rosen, Carol G. (eds.), *Studies in relational grammar*, vol. 2, 81–125. Chicago: The University of Chicago Press.

Van Valin, Robert D. Jr. & LaPolla, Randy J. 1997. *Syntax. Structure, meaning and function*. Cambridge, UK: Cambridge University Press.

Vendler, Zeno. 1957. *Linguistics in philosophy*. Ithaca: Cornell University Press.

Webelhut, Gert. 1992. *Principles and parameters of syntactic saturation*. New York: Oxford University Press.

Whitley, M. Stanley. 2002. *Spanish/English contrasts. A course in Spanish linguistics*. 2nd edn. Washington, DC: Georgetown University Press.

Index

Printed in the United States
by Baker & Taylor Publisher Services